To Mel...

2 speci

peace... forever +

I am Spirit! always

Wendy

x

WENDY SHEFFIELD

This book incorporates Wendy Sheffield's three books:
Spirit Writer
Pure Spirit; and
Spirit Healer
By putting together these three books has enabled the author to clarify
the contents therein, and to also include new material

This book is published by Spiritwriterspeaks.

A CIP record for this book is available from the British Library.

 Created with Vellum

Contents

PART THREE
SPIRIT HEALER

Foreword

This section includes a collection of endorsements of people who have read both Spirit Writer and Pure Spirit, which are encompassed within this trilogy. No endorsements are available for Spirit Healer, as this is the latest of Wendy Sheffield's books.

By putting together these three books has enabled the author to clarify the contents therein, and to also include new material. All identifies have been omitted to protect personal information.

ENDORSEMENTS FOR SPIRIT WRITER

REVIEW 1
This is a wonderfully unusual read. Honest and insightful, Wendy talks you through her personal experiences and then shares wider research. Spirit Writer is only a short read but has bundles of information and energy into this subject, I glided through the pages with intrigue and

engagement. A great starter for someone interested in this subject matter and/or may want to pursue this with a thirst for knowledge.

REVIEW 2

This is one beautiful piece of writing, I am very much into spirituality and mindfulness so I knew that I was going to enjoy this one! The author clearly has a passion when it comes to guiding others on their spiritual journey and this comes through in her writing.

I loved reading about the author's own spiritual journey and could relate to certain parts of it. This lady tells her story in a gripping and fascinating way which made me feel like the two of us had some kind of spiritual connection.

Inspiring, thought-provoking and engaging with a touch of humour here and there. This was one amazing read and I just know that it won't be long before I have a second read through!

REVIEW 3

This book is about how the writer encountered psychic experiences. These experiences seemed to have started early in childhood, and at times filled her with fear, though she says that she also had a vivid imagination. She mentions that she lived in a fantasy world at times as a child and felt that spirits were filling her head with messages which she did not understand. To combat this fear she danced incessantly to block the messages. She was shy as a child, lacking self-confidence and was bullied.

Over time she says developed psychic abilities at Sutton Coldfield Spiritualist Church and Arthur Findlay College. She writes that she is now a medium.

I like the easy read and straightforwardness and heartfelt approach to the book. Her honest account about her journey throughout her troubled childhood to early adulthood is both moving and courageous, with its trials and tribulations.

I especially enjoyed the extract by Harry Price that she has included (Part 1, Chapter 23). His approach is grounded, clear and offers comprehensive knowledge and education. He describes how difficult it is to prove anything pertaining to psychic matters in a purely material or scientific way.

On the whole this an interesting easy to read approach, explaining the writer's experience of spiritual enfoldment and subsequent knowledge and understanding.

REVIEW 4

Wendy Sheffield is a Spirit Writer who has in so many ways, walked a very challenging pathway to finally arrive at her destination, that of a person whom Spirit speaks through and with which has not come without considerable cost and turbulence.

Born to parents who lived a very traditional life, she was an only child who heard voices, had imaginary friends and vivid dreams, which to a child was somewhat terrifying. She was different and so was largely left alone at school, misunderstood by her teachers and also her parents. She taught herself to dance and found the dance floor was the only place she could be her true self.

It was not until she left school and went to Business College, she began to gain confidence, make friends and develop a skill base which was to see her become a professional in the legal world.

A marriage gone bad and a small son she loved were all part of her journey, which also came with so many lessons to be learned, understanding to be gained and revelations about the often worrying aspect of her life, that of spirit writing and her connection to Spirit.

In Spirit Writer she offers her life journey and her pathway to all who are interested in connecting with Spirit, to help them understand the journey, the connection and most importantly to have confidence in themselves to travel their pathway.

Her early journey into spirit writing was frustrating as normally this is done by hand, but as she had excellent keyboard skills eventually Spirit accepted the new form of technology as the way forward and since those early days, via Wendy and her keyboard skills, Spirit speaks freely.

Spirit Writer is not a lengthy book and can easily be read in one sitting to gain the overall message, and then used as a reference guide to further understand salient points of interest or learning.

Throughout the book, she states that the reason she is sharing her past history is to explain her journey as one of growth and healing, and to underline that at times, even though the journey can be terrifying, it is well worth undertaking. She also stresses the importance of seeking out likeminded people who can help, train and encourage, as they also act as mentors in a world that is far from familiar.

As the book concludes at a plateau, there is a second book about to be released Pure Spirit, which looks at the next level of her journey where she is learning to use her ability to work with and heal via Spirit.

Spirit Writer is an excellent piece of work which is easy and comfortable to read and will help, aid and encourage you to find your way to your true spiritual path.

REVIEW 5

I devoured Spirit Writer on a few train journeys. Although the book is very short, there is a lot of information and also a lot of content where you need to take your time to properly digest and listen to Wendy's messages and advice.

I do believe in Spirit, I do regularly attend Spirit churches, and I have had my fair share of experiences - but I wasn't aware of spirit writing as a form! I've connected with mediums, painters, but spirit writing is a totally new form to me! So it was absolutely wonderful to see that side of this and become aware of this form of mediumship.

I loved reading about Wendy's back story, and what led her to mediumship and her journey with spirits. It is a hard journey, with many dips, but Wendy sees her journey as all chances to learn and Wendy doesn't let that stop her! Sometimes we have to be in tune with ourselves and with our emotions to completely understand the situations we are in.

REVIEW 6

A delightful and honest account of an individual finding her path in spiritualism and learning about her higher self and her calling.

I really like the fact that the writer documented all her experiences including her obstacles, challenges and lessons to become a spirit writer. From understanding her early experience as a child, even losing jobs and her home to pursue her dream to become a medium.

A great read if you are new to this topic and are starting your journey of self-discovery.

REVIEW 7

Spirit Writer is a wonderful insight into how the world of spirit can work with us. Wendy Sheffield shares her story – and what a captivating story it is!

From her personal struggles with relationships and bereavement to her experiences and enlightenment attending spiritual churches. We learn through Spirit Writer that life does go on, that death is just another door we go through – a journey forward!

Having experienced the pain of losing someone close, I found Spirit Writer comforting, reassuring and also fascinating to read. It's hard to let go when someone close to you passes away, but reading this book gave me hope and comfort to think that they are still 'there' but in another form/level/plane/world. This whole topic is one of life's biggest mysteries and reading Wendy's book has given me a deeper insight. As the great Jonathan Edwards once said:

"There's no such thing as coincidence."

After reading this book, I began researching Harry Price. This is always a sign that I've enjoyed a book - when I begin researching more information! If like me, you are unfamiliar with Harry Price, this is what I researched - in a nutshell:

Harry Price: The Original Ghost Hunter (1881-1948) was a psychic researcher and famous for his investigation into the Haunting at Borley Rectory, which was, at the time, hailed the most haunted house in England. He successfully exposed a number of mediums as fraudsters, such as spiritual photographer William Hope and mediums Helen Duncan and Eileen Garrett. In 1926, Harry Price set up the National Laboratory of Psychical Research.

REVIEW 8

Spirit Writer is a highly accessible, an enjoyable insight into Wendy's spiritual journey to becoming a medium using writing to channel spirit. It covers her life experiences as well as an overview of spiritualism, providing a simple foundation to build knowledge from. Written with confidence and passion, it led us want to know more.

Everyone in the Emporium believes in the spirit world, thanks to working in a haunted building, but neither practise mediumship in the conventional sense.

Amber came into the book unaware of spirit writing or spiritualism while Willow had visited mediums and a spiritualist church soon after her mum's death. This resulted in her witnessing some fascinating readings, including a talented spirit artist so she could relate to some of Wendy's experiences.

Both found something in the book and the love and non-judgemental aspects of the church was explained well. Though spiritualism is a religion, its belief system can slot alongside other mainstream ones including the individual paths Willow and Amber follow.

Beyond Wendy's journey, *Spirit Writer* gives a background and advice on spiritual matters, including a transcript from Harry Price, famed for his investigations into fraudulent hauntings. From the spirit world, he shared his views on ghosts and manifestations. This was a fascinating, nice touch!

Both witches proceeded to analyse the Emporium's ghosts, Percy, Marley and the unknown on the stairs, to see where they fitted in.

ENDORSEMENTS FOR PURE SPIRIT

REVIEW 1

Pure Spirit is a relatively short book and took me just a couple of days to read. It's composed of a series of messages conveyed to Wendy through spirit, using her mediumistic abilities. Each message has its own chapter, breaking the whole book into easily digestible nuggets of advice and information.

From chapters entitled: In memory of my dad, The Sea of Life, Previous Lives, Spirit Wants To Speak To You, to, Do Animals Have Souls? These are fascinating topics which I enjoyed reading and have often wondered about in the past.

The messages that Wendy shares reminded me of a pack of Angel Cards which I'd bought years ago – only with Pure Spirit, there is much more information. These messages bring comfort, and encouragement.

I find the 'unknown' a fascinating topic. I've never believed in coincidences and strongly believe in fate. Having experienced bereavement myself, I find it comforting to believe that our loved ones have moved on and not simply ceased to exist. However, there will always be a certain degree of scepticism – thanks to fraudsters out there, many will remain doubtful of communication from the spirit world. I guess we'll never truly know for sure until our time is up! I'm 95% sure that there is a spirit world, and reading Pure Spirit is the closest I'll get to communicating with those on the other side.

For anyone interested in the afterlife, spirit communication and inspirational messages from beyond, then Wendy Sheffield's book is for them. I personally found the book motivating and enjoyable, not to mention enthralling!

REVIEW 2

Throughout her books, Sheffield allows us a greater insight into the world of spirit, their communication and a greater understanding of how we too can make contact with spirit. Pure Spirit is well written, definitely worth a read and is easily a one sitting book.

Books like this for me are interesting and aspiring, as

I've had previous encounters with spirit and would love to extend my reach into contacting them.

REVIEW 3

Another great little book from Wendy Sheffield.

I had the pleasure of reading Wendy's first book Spirit Writer and I found it extremely interesting.

This second book comes soon after, and again is easy to read, slim and straightforward.

I have gained so much knowledge from reading these two books, I thank Wendy for her openness and her ability to write in such detail of her spiritual experiences. A very interesting subject for me, as grieving myself and wish to connect.

If you are interested in spiritual awareness, need guidance or wish to learn more, take encouragement from these books. I found them very helpful and informative. I feel calm and hopeful!

REVIEW 4

I'm a very spiritual person so this book was right up my street, I just knew that I was meant to read it! I love getting that feeling when it comes to books! It's an indication that I myself am on the right path or that I am at least heading that way!

The author's aim here is to help the reader to connect better with their inner self, to be open to the things that cannot be seen and to encourage the reader to embrace and understand their own spiritual path and journey.

The author shares with us a variety of passages which

she hopes will help with certain situations, such as losing a loved one. The main aim seems to be to help people understand the importance and power of the written and spoken word. Words can be very powerful when used by those who know how!

Overall, this is a beautiful piece of work full of inspiration, comfort and compassion which I firmly believe could help many people!

REVIEW 5

This is a great book which I enjoyed. I do love learning about the afterlife and experiences. This book explained things like what happens when you are gone, how to control you anger and grief and learning about the afterlife. It's an interesting book.

This is book two following on from her first book Spirit Writer, in which Wendy Sheffield goes into far more detail as she sets down the purpose behind being a Spirit Writer, recounts a little of her personal journey and reaches out with love, to offer the words of her guides/spirits to all who are in need of guidance.

The Preface sets out a little of Wendy's journey but also contains a considerable amount of information about the 'Spirit' within us all; we are born with it but over the years of our lives we lose the ability, or rather hide the ability, to be able to listen to that still quiet voice and understand what we are being told.

Each of the chapters is set out with a small introduction which leads to the words of Spirit in relation to the subject matter.

The first two chapters are dedicated to her Father and then her Mother after their passing. These are beautifully worded and for those who are grieving the loss of a loved one, the graceful words in chapter 4; Spirit wants to speak to you, are perfect, offering love and comfort in a very gentle manner!

The Personal Responsibility of Words (Chapter 7) is a chapter which resonates and is one that should be read carefully, as it sets down the personal responsibility we all have for our words; spoken or written. Spirit says that it is up to all of us to teach our children wisely and well, as words are powerful, they can make or break people, portray love or hate, happiness or cruelty and so much more. Spirit offers and leaves behind much 'food for thought'.

A quirky chapter is Time (Chapter 17) especially in today's world where we never seem to have enough of it, as it 'aims to help people appreciate and value time' (sic). Very salutary!

Whereas one of the gentlest of pieces is 'Through the eyes of a wolf' (Chapter 25) which captures perfectly so much we have forgotten or overlooked.

As each of the chapters unfurl, the words flow as if a balm is being poured over the soul, full of comfort and explanation, that this gift of listening to Spirit can be once again heard and understood though various events in our everyday world.

Pure Spirit is divinely driven, and once read through, it is the perfect book to keep with you to use whenever life gets difficult, a simple but clear understanding of emotions is required, or perhaps a distinct feeling that a 'message' is there but needs translation.

Pure Spirit makes the perfect companion to Spirit Writer!

REVIEW 6

The spirit world and the physical world are closer than you think. Many people don't 'believe' in Spirit (Spirit in this context meaning the all-encompassing concept of life after death) and dismiss the healing powers of Spirit without even giving it a second thought. Others though, not only know about the powers of Spirit, but live a life guided by the other world.

Author, Wendy Sheffield, has not spent her whole lifetime working with Spirit. Her spiritual journey started with a dream 12 years ago and since then she has been working as a medium to communicate on behalf of loved ones who have passed over to the Spirit World, and likewise send back messages from those who wish to teach us.

Her second book, Pure Spirit, was communicated to her as both the title and the short chapters that make up the book. The passages, which are scribed in italics, are direct messages from Spirit with the aim of teaching each of us something new about ourselves, or our world. The passages are introduced by Wendy too, with a short summary of what the passage is about or who it is for, and sometimes how she came to communicate the subject.

Each passage is only a page or so long so they're not heavy reading. The vocabulary isn't difficult to comprehend and each chapter is direct and to the point. For example, the chapter titled 'Reflection In the Water' (Chapter 10) is about using your reflection in the water to see what others see, and explaining that what others see, might not be apparent to you until much later.

Each of the 28 chapters has something to communicate, and some of the subjects (such as death and fear of the unknown) are heavy subjects but handled delicately.

Wendy writes with soft prose as well as understanding, and hopefully her readers will pick up on her concern as well as the philosophy she is conveying.

It wouldn't matter if you are Spiritualist, merely interested in mediumship and the Spirit World or even if you are a complete non-believer, there is something in this book for everyone. Not all of the chapters are about the Spirit World or mediumship but you will learn a lot about the Spiritualist movement and teachings by reading the book cover-to-cover. For anyone needing any kind of guidance or support, such as in grieving or loss, Pure Spirit is a good place to start without getting too involved and hemmed in with technicalities.

The book lends itself, with short chapters, to being able to be picked up and put down easily, whilst being absorbed in short sprints.

Wendy Sheffield clearly loves what she does and has found her clear life path, a spiritual path, and enjoys communicating from the Spirit World to our own!

REVIEW 7

Although Pure Spirit is a short book, it doesn't stop the impact or the importance of the messages that are being put across. In fact, being short suits the tone of the book as it purely focuses on the messages themselves.

I highly recommend reading Pure Spirit if you want a nice journey into Spiritualism and reading messages that can help you in situations whether happy or sad or troubling. This is a great and insightful read and one I'll have on my bookshelves for a long time!

REVIEW 8

I reviewed Spirit Writer some time ago, left me with a lot to consider. To examine my own spirituality was never impossible but certainly was challenging. I have considered a lot since that first book and I have come to accept my version.

Pure Spirit, Wendy Sheffield's second book is a book that intends to connect you with messages from spirit in order to guide you on a path of acceptance and fulfilment. It is a unique book with an interesting pretence.

I have been flitting in and out of Pure Spirit. Reading it out of order - don't say a thing! Tabbing, highlighting and responding to what resonates with me. I am savouring every session, every moment I spend in this book. There are valuable insights here.

The book is written well - Wendy allows spirit to flow through her so I'm thinking spirit knows what they're doing. This book touches upon many issues: death, loneliness, grief and even words.

I have enjoyed flitting in and out of this book. I have considered the words within and I have come to the conclusion that there is value in Wendy's (and spirit's) words. I believe that each reader will close the book with a different outcome. We will all get something different from it - that is the joy of interpretation!

REVIEW 9

Pure Spirit is for anyone who is interested in the concept of the afterlife, who attends or is considering attending a spiritualist church, who has been to see a medium or psychic, who believes it is possible to communicate with spirit.

It is ideal for "newbies" who want to learn more about spirit communication, and who wish to be inspired by how another person communicates with spirit and interprets their messages.

The author, Wendy Sheffield, changed her life 12 years ago and writes openly about the influence of her grandma talking to her in her dreams. She wrote and released her first book Spirit Writer in 2022, as more of a memoir / background to her life and discovery of spiritualism. Pure Spirit is a quick read; a series of short passages combining messages from spirit (in italics) with context and sometimes interpretation from Wendy.[Both books are now included in this new book 'I Am Spirit!']

If you're not interested in the afterlife, the bigger picture, if you don't ask questions like do animals have souls and what happens when you die then this is not a book for you. But for those interested in finding out more about spirit and an insight into how a person learns to communicate with spirit this is a fascinating read!

REVIEW 10

If you have ever been curious about the afterlife, about spirits and spirituality then this is definitely a book for you. I found this to be such an interesting read.

Wendy Sheffield, the author, shares with us a range of different messages and communications from spirit and each of these has its own chapter within the book, which, along with a nice writing style, make this a good book to read.

I personally am very intrigued by the afterlife, so I devoured this book in no time at all, and it has motivated me to explore other resources to find out more.

I definitely recommend this book.

PART ONE
Spirit Writer

I AM SPIRIT!

From the moment of our birth and throughout the whole of our lives, we soon recognize that we are all judged by others, rightly or wrongly, This misguided judgment of others soon clouds our dreams until they appear to disappear into the ether, leaving an empty space inside you!

It is not until we have tragedy in our lives do we start to look for answers as to why certain things happen. When we start to question the whys in our lives, we often start to accept that there is a higher existence that guides humanity. The inner beliefs that we had as a child secretly grow within us like a seed ready to flourish when the time is right for us. When we start to feel this inner yearning we start to realize that we are NOT alone and we begin to recognize our spirit within. It was at this point that my true spiritual journey started when I acknowledged that 'I Am Spirit!'

When the time was right for me, I was able to discover

who exactly I was, but to do this I had to consider all the strange occurrences that had happened throughout my life. Spirit had never let me forget my life journey, and I did not understand why until I had both the time and energy to discover the same. When that moment arrived, I was encouraged by spirit to write my first book Spirit Writer, which tells my life story of how spirit came into my life and helped me sort out a lifetime's worth of misinformation given to me by others.

When I learned to understand and recognize my path, my mediumship improved and I began to realize that I was channeling spirit messages to guide people. It was at this time that I wrote Pure Spirit.

Finally, part of my spiritual path was to learn about healing and accept that I was a spiritual healer. It was at this time that I wrote Spirit Healer to help people understand the true beauty of healing and recognize that alternative methods of healing have been around for generations.

When I completed these three short books to help guide people on their spiritual journeys, I was later reminded that all three books were meant to be put together to make one book. This was the start of this my latest book which has given me an opportunity to rewrite and answer questions that many of my readers have put to me, and also given me the opportunity to update my readers with the latest spiritual events in my life.

Spirit helped me transform my life so that I could discover my true spiritual beauty within, and I hope that this book will help you discover your inner beauty too!

For my grandmother, Florence Marjorie Canning

CHAPTER 1

New Beginnings

I started my journey as an ordinary lady who spent her life dreaming of being a psychic medium only to discover, after a lifetime's worth of strange occurrences and spirit messages, that I was one – not just any psychic medium, but one that could spirit write using a keyboard!

I hope that by following my journey you too will consider your spiritual side of life. You might recognise gut feelings that often come true, or you might hear inner voices that you are scared to share with the world in case you might be mocked. It was feelings like this that made me believe in myself and discover my true spiritual path, which is to understand my own unfoldment so that I could help others with theirs. With the aid of my newfound mediumistic ability, I was also able to unravel a family mystery going back generations which had caused disharmony amongst them.

In the beginning, I thought I was just imagining what

I had heard, but as my life progressed I started to believe and accept my spiritual journey. It did, however, take a great deal of evidence for me to believe the spirit messages that I was receiving, which included visiting several world class mediums to check my messages. Much to my surprise, everything in these readings confirmed what spirit had told me!

I have provided two chapters where I consider the evidence that I have of strange occurrences and predictions that I experienced along my journey (Chapters 15 and 16). It was only when I stood up to the outside world about my beliefs that I discovered my true spiritual journey. I now invite you to discover your journey!

My motto is 'Believe And You Will Achieve' which basically means if you believe in yourself, you will gain the confidence to achieve whatever your heart desires!

CHAPTER 2

What is spirit writing?

I thought it important to start with a description of what spirit writing is. The traditional method of spirit writing is by using a pen and paper. The medium keeps an open mind whilst holding the pen and permits spirit to control her hand, allowing spirit to attempt to write messages which can later be deciphered. This is not to be confused by the term 'ghost writer' where an author appoints a person to write on their behalf.

When trying to spirit write yourself, it is important to be comfortable and to clear your mind and not to worry about anything. Some people find that music can help them relax. Many automatic writers find that music with vocals can influence their writing, so be cautious in your choice of background tunes. It is important to ground yourself and clear your brain of thoughts and put your pen to paper. Your wrist should be limp whilst you are holding your pen, you are trying to encourage spirit to work through you. Just write the first thing that comes to mind and then keep going. As words pop into your brain, allow your hand to freely write without thinking about what you are writing.

Don't worry about trying to interpret what you have written just yet. Figuring out the meaning is something to do when you're all finished. Some people find that asking a specific question is a good way to get the flow started. You can simply write the question on your paper and then see what sort of responses come out. If the answers you're writing don't seem to correspond to your question, don't worry, write them anyway. Often, we get answers to the questions we *didn't* ask. Keep going until it seems like the words have stopped. For some people this can be after ten minutes, for others it can be an hour. Some people like to use a timer, so they don't find themselves sitting at a table all afternoon scribbling things out. After you've finished, it's time to review what you have written. Look for patterns, words, themes that resonate with you. For instance, if you see repeated references to work or jobs, it's possible you need to focus on matters relating to your employment. Watch for names. If you see names you don't recognize, it's possible that you are taking a message for someone else. You may even find pictures such as doodles, characters, or symbols, etc. Keep in mind that your results may be neat and orderly, or they may be chaotic and all over the place. It is important, as with all forms of psychic divination, to practice automatic writing, the more you'll come to understand the messages you are receiving from the other side.

When I first became aware of my spirit writing, spirit

tried to work through me using the traditional method of pen and paper. When spirit became aware that I was struggling to keep up with this, they then encouraged me to spirit write using a keyboard – a skill which they knew I had the whole of my life. This, therefore, allowed me to keep up with the spirit communication in a way with which I was familiar. It took a while before I realised that spirit was trying to communicate through me in this way, but when I learned to exercise control, my messages flowed freely, and I am now able to use this skill to discover new directions for my life as well as guiding other people with their lives, which I love to do!

Spirit will constantly try to communicate with you, which means that you do have to be extremely vigilant in what messages you are receiving in your mind and what is happening to your body. It was by being vigilant with how spirit was working with me that I realised they were using my skill as a fast typist. It is with this newfound skill that I finally discovered a way in which I could finally communicate with the world!

* * *

CHAPTER 3

What is Spiritual Unfoldment?

Spiritual unfoldment often occurs when someone has gone through a tragic circumstance in their life. In my case, it occurred when I was going through a divorce. It often makes someone more attuned to spirit, meaning that they become more sensitive and may start to see, hear or sense spirit. When you start to spiritually unfold, you begin to understand your spiritual existence which helps you realise who you are and what your personal journey is. When someone acknowledges the existence of spirit in their lives it often makes them hungry to know more. By accepting spirit into your life, it allows your spirit guides to guide you in their everyday life. After acknowledgment of the same, you will find that your spiritual awareness will grow which will enable you to communicate and connect to spirit and your guides. From that moment on, you will begin to realise the important things in life and want to help your fellow mankind.

The first step to unfoldment is to recognise that there

is a 'higher self' which you want to know more about. Your interest in spirit will then allow them to assist you on your journey. They will not be able to help you with your life unless you give them permission to do so, however.

There are many examples of stories of people in the public domain about people who have a clear understanding of spiritual unfoldment or spiritual awakening. One such gentleman is:

Eckhart, T (2020) He was educated at the Universities of London and Cambridge, and he regularly gives his opinion on what he believes is happening around the world on YouTube. He talks about his life journey of self-discovery which started at the age of 29 where he began a profound inner transformation that radically changed the course of his life. He invites people to start their path towards awakening to find who they truly are by considering his journey. He claims that "awakening to happiness" is happening to many individuals around the world which is drawing them to spiritual teachings as it is their awakening. He talks about how it is important to understand who you are and asks you consider how the world sees you now and in the future.

Arthur Findlay College (2018) We will now consider the views of two of Arthur Findlay College mediums who, in one of their workshops, also considered why 'unfoldment' or 'awakening' is taking place. They suggest that there is obviously something much bigger going on in the world due to the increasing need of people seeking guidance from psychics and mediums rather than using traditional methods for guidance. They have come to this conclusion from listening to many people who have come to them for readings. They suggest that something has awakened within us, or something has happened so that we are made aware of spirit around us and because of this we get an awakening and "get the bug". Because of this awakening, we become aware of our own spirit and consequently spirit is attracted to us to provide encouragement, making you feel like you are "piggy in the middle". Once you feel this way, you believe you have a sense of why you are doing something which motivates you and allows you to understand your inner drive. They also talk about what is happening in the world today and why people are looking for answers now. They suggest that many people are searching online hoping to find the answer to what life is all about. They suggest that spirit wants to help mankind to teach people about the eternity of life. They suggest that spirit wants to make us aware of the spirit within us. They suggest that spirit wants to remove limitations and wants to expand our understanding, and from this you realise that there is a bigger plan unfolding. They suggest that spirit, despite wanting to help us, are not there to gratify us. They explain to us that if spirit do not come through, you should consider whether you are using the right medium or whether it might not be time to come through for that spirit. Another reason why certain spirits do not come through is because someone else needs to come through with a higher priority. Spirit wants to help us to understand that we are not "mortal" and they want to lead us to God. They explain that spiritualism is a now a recognised religion in the UK and spirit will lead us to divine power.

After considering these two accounts, clearly more people are searching for guidance from mediums and psychics to help with their lives because they are not getting answers from traditional methods. With the aid of the internet, people are now able to search for answers in a way in which they were never able to before. This is exactly what happened to me when I was seeking guidance to solve issues within my life. I felt I had no-one to turn to help me understand what I was experiencing. Everyone that I spoke to before I discovered spiritualist churches were all telling me that everything was 'all in my mind'. It did not matter how often I was told this, I just would not accept this as I felt deep down that my experiences were 'real'.

Along my path, I did not find it easy to find spiritual guidance and used to have countless readings from mediums when at times I could not really afford to do so. I desperately wanted answers, and I would listen to anybody and everybody!

In my quest for answers, I discovered The Leslie Flint Trust (1997-2022). Leslie Flint was a well-recognised medium, well known for his many voice box recordings. These recordings helped me to understand the Spirit World in more detail, which includes the fact that the lower level of the Spirit World is where people go to on their passing. They will be given a chance to consider their lives, and they will experience how their life impacted on other people's lives. They will also be given the chance to stop at this level or whether to progress to higher levels, where they no longer crave Earthly possessions. In spirit, you will have the same characteristics as you did on the Earthly plane.

There are now people in the world who can give guidance on spirit happenings. Nobody needs to be scared to talk about spiritual issues any longer. However, you do still need to be mindful to talk to people who have knowledge of the same, as there are still many doubters in the world – people who are scared, people who want to follow the crowd in their understandings and beliefs. There are still many people who 'fear' hearing voices. They should be embracing their inner voice and not fear the same.

Some of the spirits that came through Leslie Flint admitted that they were scared to tell people in their time that they were getting their inspiration from spirit!

There are also many things that can hold you back when you are trying to unfold. Lack of knowledge breeds fear, and that is why it is important not to listen to the wrong people when learning about spiritualism. It is important to surround yourself with love, love from spirit and love from people who understand about spirit.

To improve your knowledge of spiritualism, I would suggest that you visit a local Spiritualist Church as a starting point, read books by recognised people in the field and have readings by the many gifted mediums in the world today, such as those on the Arthur Findlay College website. They provide two types of readings evidential and assessment. The 'evidential' is a link to your loved ones and the assessment is a 'spiritual assessment' where the medium links to your spirit guides for guidance on your spiritual journey and abilities. It was from one of these assessments that I was able to confirm elements of my own journey. I was not just willing to accept my own spirit messages, I wanted confirmation from world-class recognised mediums. My experience in the legal profession had taught me to get proof to back up information.

After two unfoldments, I was completely sure of my spiritual journey, which was to understand my own unfoldment so that I could help others with theirs.

I hope that you will not be scared to ask for guidance to help you discover your true spiritual path. Remember, everyone can ask spirit for guidance at any time. You do have to learn to trust your messages though, which is not easy, and that is the reason I used to get readings to back up what spirit were telling me.

CHAPTER 4

Childhood

I was born on 7th September 1965, a Virgo, to a normal, average couple who had worked all their lives.

My parents had no educational background themselves, so consequently they could only help with my education as far as they were able. They were caring parents, but it was obvious that their judgments were based on their background. They were steadfast in their beliefs, with no imagination. They were also not religious in any way, and could not understand why I was always talking about God. It was clear that they had respect for the church as an institution, but they did not need religion in their life like I did. I remember hearing them talk about me from my bedroom upstairs, saying that they were worried about my obsession with God. I used to listen intently to what they said, but I did not let their opinions get in the way of what I believed in. I was steadfast in my belief, even from a young age, but I did not know why. I just accepted my belief without question.

At school, teachers were quick to notice my lack of confidence, but did not question this or offer any advice as to how to help me. This subsequently had an impact on my communication skills and my schoolwork. I believe now that even if I had had better communication skills to be able to tell my parents what was going on in my head at that time, they would not have taken me seriously. Their beliefs were tied to their parents' beliefs, and that is how the world turns now. Many people are tied to their past and scared of having their own thoughts and beliefs for fear of them being challenged and not being accepted by the world around them.

As a child, I had a wild, vivid imagination. I used to hide under the bedclothes, be scared about what was under my bed. You might say that this is normal for a child, but in my case my fear meant that I was experiencing things that only certain people could have understood and helped me with. I realise now that I was letting my own imagination scare me and that this hindered my development. My fear followed me for most of my adult life.

It wasn't until my second unfoldment, many years later, that Sutton Cold!eld Spiritualist Church helped me realise I had been listening to spirit all my life and I had been shutting out the noise in my head by constantly listening to music. My mother also should not have let me watch those horror films as a child either, as they certainly did not help – they just scared me even more. I would add here that the problem with horror films is that they infect the true message of spirituality by providing false information.

Living in a fantasy world also impacted on my life. It was in these dreams that I began my journey of communicating with spirit who I now realise filled my head with information trying to guide me in my life but unfortunately at the time I did not recognise that my visions were in fact guidance from spirit. One spirit dream that stands out for me is when I was told the name of my future husband and that he would treat me badly. As I did not realise where these messages were coming from, nor the significance they would have on my life, I did not listen to the same and subsequently I would try to block them out and forget them – only to be reminded of them years later by spirit to make sense of my journey.

I must add here that there is a difference between normal dreams and spirit dreams, which is what I had occasionally. When you have a spirit dream, you never forget it. I still remember mine from 12 years ago, but ordinary dreams come and go overnight. I would suggest that you have a notebook and pen at the side of your bed just in case you have a significant dream, as spirit often talk to people in their dreams, even if they are not a medium!

Part of my living in a dreamworld involved shutting myself in my bedroom as I felt that was my 'haven'. Consequently, I became an extremely scared, quiet child, not able to tell the world what I was experiencing. No-one knew what was in my head because I had not learnt how to release the same by communication.

Now, I must address the issue of my incessant dancing

as a child, which I now recognise as my attempt to block spirit messages from my mind because I was scared.

My father would hear my tiny feet stomping on the floor above him when he was trying to watch television or read his newspaper. I now know that I was trying to block out the noise in my head of spirit communication, and I consequently became obsessed with dancing, to the detriment of my schoolwork. All the world could see was that I was 'quiet' and that I was a good dancer, which two facts contradicted each other, but were not questioned. If ever you recognise this contradictory behaviour in your child, you should seek guidance, as this was a tell-tale sign for me that I had communication issues which stayed with me most of my life. Spotting unusual behaviour early is important with children.

On the dance floor, I could be who I wanted to be, and no-one questioned how dancing might have had had an impact on my schoolwork. The fact that I was so quiet was also not questioned. What people did notice was that I was an excellent dancer, so I continued with dancing, stomping my little feet wherever I could. The dance floor was the only place that I felt happy at that time of my life, the only place I could retreat into my little world. No-one made the connection between my dancing and my quietness. My obsession with dancing consequently had an impact on my schoolwork, but that didn't worry me, as I lived for dancing and did not think about my future. How could I think about my future when I had so much happening inside my head?

When people saw me for the first time on a dancefloor, they thought I had been taking dancing lessons, which of course I hadn't, because my parents would not have been able to afford them. I now know what I was doing was blocking out messages in my head, and I also now believe that I was learning about energies surrounding my body and learning to communicate with my higher self. Remember, I did not know what spirit was at this time and I was too young to understand that I was a medium. Despite this, I have always had an inner 'knowing' of matters without having experience of the same. I only recognise such things now because, much later in life, spirit made me aware that they had been encouraging me to remember the whole of my life to relay my story to others.

Even though I did not understand my experiences as a child, I believed in what I felt, which appeared real to me! However, I could not tell anyone about what I was experiencing, as I was so scared. I believe that if I had of trusted my inner voice at that time it might have stopped me making mistakes in my life which led me down the wrong path. However, it is hard to talk about what you do not understand, so it is important to realise that children need help interpreting their thoughts and beliefs as these can hold them back if they are scared. That's what happened to me. It is important to consider what they say, even if this does not appear to make sense, as they could be sensing spirit like I did. If this is the case, you will need to visit a Spiritualist Church because the medical profession does not accept such things! I did not believe in my inner voices as a child, so consequently I did not follow the advice that I was given, and this subsequently led me down the wrong pathway.

Apart from devoting my time to dancing, I have very bad eyesight which also affected my confidence and held me back. My glasses used to be so thick that they pulled my head down, making me appear more shy than I was. I can remember being too scared to tell my teachers when I couldn't see things in class, but in hindsight, I do not understand why I was scared to tell others of my sight issues. Teachers should have questioned why I was so quiet and recognised that I was crying out for help. The only way that I had learnt to communicate with the world at this time was through dance. I was also bullied at school and I became aware that rumours were being circulated around my school about my parents, due to jealousy, and for some reason those rumours were being believed by my classmates. This was also another reason why I was quiet. I was not brave or strong enough to stand up to my bullies, so I just retreated further into my own little world, my fantasy world, where no-one could hurt me!

My final hurdle was that I was not aware as a child that I was developing into a medium, and that the inner voices inside my head was the voice of spirit trying to guide me with my life. If I had believed this, I now know that my life would have taken a different direction. However, in my case, even if my parents had understood or believed what was happening to me, that I was developing into a medium, I believe they would not have known where to get help!

It is important for parents to recognise if their child is

not fitting in with the surroundings that they are in, as they might not get the help that they need until many years down the line. There is also a risk that a child may be misdiagnosed as having mental health issues, as doctors seem to be fearful when people say that they are listening to 'voices' in their head. Why are doctors so scared of people listening to their own voice?

It is hard for some people to accept that spirit exists around us.. I have tried to talk to my sister about messages from our deceased mother, but I can see the non-acceptance on her face!

Another issue with children is that they learn from the actions and words of their parents, so if their parents are blocking themselves from accepting spirit, they might – without intention – off-load their disbelief onto their children. Also, if children are brave enough to talk about anything to do with the spirit, their parents might not know where to get help. I would suggest going to your local Spiritualist Church for such matters.

I now recognise that my main issues as a young child were that I feared what was inside my head and this subsequently held me back for many years because I had to understand everything myself before I could help others!

When a child is quiet and unable to communicate, for whatever reason, this can hinder their life. Therefore, it is the duty of parents to try to look out for anything that might be holding their child back. My tell-tale signs were my incessant dancing and quietness, which consequently led to my lack of self-belief. I believe that if someone had encouraged me to talk as a child, then I would not have had so many life problems. My story might have been hard to understand, but it was my life, and what was in my head appeared real to me!

The moral of my story is that we must all listen to each other's stories, no matter how far-fetched they may be, as you never know what the truth is until you hear it, and consider it for what it is! You cannot put spiritual experiences in a box, they are different for everyone, and that is why it is important that they are talked about, to prevent fear. There may be similarities with psychic phenomena, but experiences are individual and subjective, which is why they need to be talked about!

I end my childhood memories by struggling to cope in secondary school due to my communication problems and not recognising that my inner voice was trying to guide me with my life journey. I did not start to understand this until I went to college, where people started to believe in my abilities.

Parents and teachers are in positions of trust so they should make themselves aware of what is normal for the child over which they have control. Remember, every child's experience of life is different, and if they off-load to parents or teachers that something has unsettled them, they should seek help on behalf of the child.

CHAPTER 5

My college days

I fondly remember my college days as happy ones, and the beginning of when I started to believe in myself and develop into a confident young lady. I don't remember any spiritual messages during that period, but what I do remember is a few strange occurrences which at the time had no rational explanation. I never questioned these strange occurrences because I recognised that no one would believe me! How could I convince others when I did not even understand what was happening myself!

After finishing secondary school, I felt demoralised when I only got a couple of GCSEs. From somewhere, I got the idea that I wanted to be a secretary, so I embarked on a Private Secretarial Course at Sutton Cold!eld College. Looking back, as my confidence was low at that time, I was not in the best place to make a life-changing decision.

With my smartest suit on, I went to an interview to be enrolled on this course, but I was told that I could only be accepted if there was a spare space at the time of the induction. It was clear that the teacher in charge was only taking in Sutton Cold!eld's grammar school girls with a string of qualifications to their names, but I was determined not to let this stop me from gaining a place.

The induction day arrived, and I was delighted when I was allowed to join the course. The class was small, with very attentive teachers who obviously loved their job. I made loads of friends who had better qualifications than myself and my confidence grew day by day. I also won the hearts of my teachers who said that I was an excellent example to the rest of the class!

During that time, everything came so easily to me, which was strange considering how I had struggled at school. Due to my increased self-belief in my abilities, I consequently passed every exam, except a couple of the more advanced ones. I sailed through my first year of the course because I had teachers and friends who believed in me and gave me the confidence to succeed. My newfound self-belief bore fruit and inspired me to fight the good fight with this career. My success proves the value of having good teachers and friends to share experiences with. All students are different, and they all require different environments and methods of teaching.

One of the main subjects on this course was shorthand, and I remember that this class was always fast and furious. We were being trained to be accurate transcribers of information. We would first be given a passage to learn and then our teacher would read out the passage which we had to write in shorthand. We then had to transcribe the same passage as quickly as possible – timed by her.

One day something odd occurred. As usual, we were called upon to learn a passage and once we had all written it in Pitman Shorthand, the teacher would go around class and ask her students to read out what they had written. I was chosen on one occasion, but instead of reading out the contents of the passage, strange words came out of my mouth. The teacher tried to get her stopwatch out, but she did not bother to use it, obviously not believing what she had heard! What I consider was strange about this incident is that she never questioned my behaviour on that day, nor did any of my friends (of which there were many) ask me what had been going on!

I have been trying to understand what happened that day for years and the only conclusion I have come to is that I was speaking tongues. I have since researched the meaning of this. In *The Bible Acts 2:4*, speaking in tongues is initial evidence or sign of the baptism of the Holy Spirit.

'And they were filled with the Holy Ghost, and began to speak with other tongues, as the Spirit gave them utterance.'

Exam time came around quickly, and we were all entered for many exams in order that we could gain as many qualifications as possible. My secondary school had not taught me how to prepare for exams, but my college did, and I felt fully prepared and equipped for anything that would come my way. They taught me the importance

of working through past papers which is the most important thing that any student should do.

During the period of my exams, I experienced another
odd occurrence. This happened during a particular three-
hour exam. I started the paper and then appeared to put
myself in some sort of trance. When I came out of the
trance, I found that the three allotted hours were over.
This happened a few times at college. Although I can
remember these occurrences clearly, I did not understand
their significance at the time, but I never forgot what
happened, as it was so strange!

I sailed through my first year at college and gained a
vast array of qualifications. They trained us hard, and I
responded well to the good teaching and small classes.

During the second year of college, I met my ex-
husband, so my attention was slightly steered towards him
rather than studying. This didn't matter so much as I had
worked so hard in my first year that my lapse of attention
on this second year did not really matter. My teachers were
concerned at my slight dip in grades, but this concern was
proved to be unfounded as I had worked hard enough in
my first year to carry me through. I appeared to no longer
have the communication issues that I had as a child. My
teachers believed in me, and my parents were proud that I
had succeeded in preparing myself for a worthwhile career.

At the end of this course, the lady who had inter-
viewed me two years before, who did not want to take me
on the course, now relayed her apologies as I was the only
student in the class that had passed everything.which was

incredible considering my fellow students were all more qualified than I was.

With a trail of qualifications in my back pocket and my new-found con!dent personality, I went out into the big wide world with renewed vigour!

CHAPTER 6

My working life

My collection of qualifications and my new-found confidence gained me a good career within the legal profession, which lasted over 20 years. However, despite my success I could never understand why I was never satisfied and would continually feel the need to jump from job to job. This habit started to make my cv harder and harder to explain, because I did not understand my behaviour myself. I also did not understand why, even after a full day at work, I would still want to race home, searching for new life directions – not just career-wise, but in relationships, too!

As time passed, I recognised that when I was respected by a firm I was working for, people noticed I was capable of so much more and would question why I was still a secretary. But when I was working for firms that did not respect me, I became totally bored and struggled to even do the most mundane secretarial work. Another reason that I was at times unhappy was that I would often find myself victim to ruthless people, due to my sensitive nature and would end up leaving firms even when I enjoyed the job. I had a big heart, and I was used and abused in the city by a lot of ruthless people.

Despite whether I felt happy or unhappy where I worked, it was clear that I was always loved and respected by the people that I worked with, which I did not discover until years later. I believe this was because over the years I had learnt how to treat people and even though I was ambitious I would never tread on anyone's toes. Years later, one of my work colleagues came back through a medium to tell me how much she respected me. This touched me, as I believed I had never had time for friends due to the busy environment I worked in. This lady had remembered me and came back through a medium to relay her love and respect years later.

When I reflect on the various managers that I worked for throughout my career, I noticed that I seemed to have better relations with managers when I was working close to them – something I could not understand. I now know that I was using my psychic ability to climatize myself, not only with my manager, but also with the whole firm. Some of my managers would often wonder how I knew things, which I could not explain. I had wild ideas in my head that I must be psychic, but it was many years after that I discovered that I was. I now appreciate the importance of managers who believe in your abilities and how important it is to protect one's vulnerability from ruthless people.

My last manager was the best I had ever had. He believed in me, but when I ran into difficulties he could not fight my corner because I had written him an email using my spirit writing, which concerned him. No-one understood my spirit writing at that time, so no-one could help me. I know that it hurt him to let me go as he recognised the connection that we had. However, only I knew that our connection was a spiritual one which would have been hard for him to understand as solicitors are not allowed to believe in spiritual matters!

I lost my last two jobs due to my spirit writing. My employers both tried to help me, but decided they could not, as it seemed my personal life was too mixed up. At this time I could not control what I was saying or writing, which meant I was misunderstood.

Despite losing my career in the legal profession, I had gained some valuable skills which would stay with me for the rest of my life. The skills that I had gained using my hands over the years were later used by spirit to communicate with the world!

Due to my mixed up personal life I could no longer hold down a job in the legal profession which lead to my becoming ill. My ex-husband tried to force me back into work despite us both being told that I should not return to work. His intimidation during a difficult time in my life made me realise that I had to divorce and make a new life for myself. I had supported him the whole of our marriage life when he was ill, but the one time I was ill, he would not support me!

* * *

CHAPTER 7

Motherhood

I was working at Anthony Collins Solicitors in Birmingham when I discovered I was pregnant with my son. I collapsed on a bus on the way to work, and after medical examinations I was told that I was six months pregnant. This was a tremendous shock to the whole of my family because they all knew how much I valued my career and that I was not planning to have children. What they did not know was that I had an inner yearning for a child, without even realising it. This is an example of why you should always listen to what your body is telling you, as it has a voice of its own!

The morning after I collapsed, I noticed that my belly seemed to have grown overnight. I instantly accepted what was ahead, as I knew that this was meant to be. The first thought in my head was: who was I not to give this child a chance in life?

During the same period, I experienced a strange occurrence at this firm. After notifying Human Resources of my pregnancy, the senior partner approached me and put his hands on my tummy and said, 'God bless you.' I thought this very odd at the time, but I have pondered on this and all I can come up with is that he saw my light, just like my grandmother did. Why else would a senior partner of a large firm in the city do such a thing? I now realise that for him to make a spiritual connection with me meant that he must have been a very special man himself.

The lead-up to my taking maternity leave was a happy time in my life. I was excited to meet up with my work colleagues and enjoyed listening to other mother's experiences. I finally had a common interest to share! I confessed how scared I was about having a child and one friend reassured me that there would be lots of people around me at the hospital helping me at the birth. This comment gave me all the reassurance that I needed!

I had my son one month early. As I only discovered that I was pregnant at six months, I was only aware of his existence for 2 months! I had a difficult birth, which was mainly fuelled by my fear of labour – something I know many women will relate to. After a long labour, the midwife suggested that forceps be used, but I would not allow this, as I had heard too many bad stories about forceps damaging the baby's head. Instead, I begged them to do a C-section, which they did.

I was high on gas and air at the time and would not let go of the receptacle because I was so scared. I was subsequently moved to the operating theatre to have my C-section, and whilst on the operating table, I could feel blood leaving my body. I remember spirit approaching me and I said deep within my mind that I would die for my son and spirit replied that it was not my time! I now believe that this was a near-death experience for me.

On 11th November 1997, my son Alex was born. He was tiny, but perfect in every way. From the moment I held him in one hand, I could feel the potential of this little man. He was my own 'little star', who put me in favour again with my ex-husband for a short time. I now recognise that I had feared giving birth to a child and that was the reason for my denial of wanting a child until then.

My maternity leave came and went. These days, women get a year, but at the time I had my son I was only allowed two months maternity leave. I had to finish work a month before my maternity leave was due because I was suffering with backache, so in the end I only had one month's maternity leave.

Like all new mothers, I enjoyed my maternity leave, pottering around my house, doing jobs that I never normally had time to do because I was always working, and I was often too tired to do anything when I got home. I would have loved to continue being a 'stay at home' mom but my ex-husband encouraged me to return, so back to work I went with a heavy heart!

Time passed quickly and before long my son was a toddler. I found it frustrating when he couldn't talk to me, but I knew I had to be patient as every parent needs to be with a young child. Parents should remember that just because children cannot talk does not mean they are not receptive of what is being said to them. When he did start to talk, it was amazing. I was truly a proud mother and I paid close attention to anything he was having problems with so that he would not encounter the same hurdles in his life that I had.

I noticed that from a young age he had problems holding a pen, but I did not know at the time how to help him with this. I also recognised that he was a quiet child, as I had been. I realised that I needed to address this because I was only too aware how communication issues had impacted on my life, and I did not want the same for him. To address this, I found a local football team for young- sters, where he immediately fitted in. All his friends loved him and he proved to be quite the little star on the football pitch! His grandfather would occasionally, when he was well, go along to watch and cheer him on. After joining the team, my son's communication skills developed in spades, and it was clear he had a mind of his own from a young age!

My son had changed my life forever. I was now a mellower person, and it was clear that my life would never return to how it had been, and I didn't want it to!

CHAPTER 8

*Mistakes people made
about me*

Before losing two positions in the legal profession, I was sent on numerous occasions to sit before various doctors to diagnose me. The first time was before a team of doctors, with my dear departed father alongside me. My father tried to tell them that he believed it was the conditions in which I lived which had impacted on my mental health, but they would not listen to him. They ordered him out of the room and continued to scare me with their pre-conditioned questions. Unfortunately, as I was so afraid, I could not speak clearly so I was misdiagnosed with a mental health condition.

Years later, a nurse who had been in the group at the time, visited my house and told me that there had been arguments amongst them when they were trying to diagnose me. Some of the team had apparently questioned why I was repeatedly saying the same things again and again, which they believed meant something. However, the head doctor wouldn't listen to his team and his misdiagnosis of my having a mental health condition stayed with me – not only in a thick file but plastered across my life thereafter. I knew that their diagnosis meant that I would never work again in the 'material' world. I also knew there was no point questioning this, so I just accepted it, and put it to the back of my mind. I might have lost my career, but no one could stop me believing that spirit was now working with me!

The many things which my doctors should have considered about me included my troubled childhood, losing my career in the legal profession and the imminent breakdown of my marriage. I also had spirit encounters, but I knew they would not have listened to this! I now realise that even if I had been able to communicate to the world when I was young or when I was before a team of doctors that misdiagnosed me, it is doubtful whether they would have listened to what I had to say. They had a list of pre-conditioned questions before them, based on the diagnosis of previous patients, and it was obvious that they would not consider anything else 'outside the box'. I believe that these kinds of misdiagnoses frequently happen due to the medical profession's inability to understand 'spiritual' matters and the connection to man's physical existence.

*'The spirit existence can live without the physical ('death'),
but the physical existence cannot exist without the spirit!'*

What was not normal to the real world was normal to me! Spiritual work was now part of my life, and I did not really care whether people believed me or not! I now believed in my mediumistic abilities, and I was determined to continue with my new-found spiritual path.

No one should be scared to stand up for what they believe in! Your beliefs are yours! Do not let anyone tell you different!

CHAPTER 9

My experience of being homeless

I had never experienced homelessness before; this was my first time. I had lost my job and my family due to my spiritual encounters. I knew that I could no longer stay in the matrimonial home as there were too many bad vibes floating around between my ex-husband and myself. We had widespread plumbing issues around our house at that time, which made me wonder if they were the result of poltergeist activity, but I could not prove this. I have provided a chapter on ghost activity, which includes poltergeist activity, to help readers consider the same. Years later,

Due to my desperation, the local council managed to secure temporary accommodation for myself at a hotel in Edgbaston which had dedicated a wing to homeless people. When I learned of my placement, I threw my clothes and limited possessions into two suitcases and jumped into the back of a taxi. I told the taxi driver to keep my location private as I was scared my ex-husband would follow me to my new location. He had done that before when he was trying to discover where I had been going to when I visited Sutton Spiritualist Church at the time of my first unfoldment.

I did not tell anyone where I had run away to, not even my parents. I needed time to sort myself out and I knew my parents would understand this.

I arrived like a gypsy, dishevelled, and shaking. After filling in a long form for benefit purposes, I was directed to my new home – one tiny room. Although I was frightened, I felt safe there, as I was finally free of my ex-husband's control. I set up my computer on my desk and carried on with my journey of self-discovery without interference from the outside world. I continued to sort out my Earthly problems, one by one, and kept working on my confidence building and self- discovery. Although I was hoping to make some friends at my new 'home', the people that were there had troubles of their own and appeared not want to make friends, so I decided to keep myself to myself.

One night, a very troubled lady, with mental health issues, knocked on my door and begged me to give her money to return to her partner. I quickly concluded that I should not help her as he had been violent towards her. I also had to pull the telephone line out of the wall as I was receiving scary telephone calls from fellow residents.

Although it was quite frightening living in an environment full of people with mental health, drink, and drug issues, it was not as scary as the vibes that had been floating around my matrimonial home.

Time passed quickly whilst I was there. I plodded along day by day, filling my time sorting out my Earthly problems. I knew spirit were with me, as I would frequently get images of numbers on hotel doors in my mind when spirit was warning me that the hotel would be moving me into other rooms. I now trusted the visions that I had, and I would never doubt them again!

One example of a vision that I had whilst I was living at the hotel/hostel included seeing a male friend on the bow of a ship, feeling very happy and content, as he looked out to sea. He confirmed what I said, but he had problems taking the ship. I explained to him that the ship represented his life journey. Another vision from my past was where I saw myself in the hotel room where I was now living.

After being in my small hotel room for approximately three months, a lady banged on my door and pushed herself into my tiny room. She told me I had to get out and she threw my meagre possessions into my suitcases and told me to leave. What people do not realise is that when a homeless person is provided with temporary accommodation they can only stop there for a short period of time.

I remember seeing one lady returning to being homeless with her meagre possessions in black bags and thinking how sad it was. Fortunately, I did have a lifeline as I knew that my parents would help me if I was desperate, and I was! They did not have a spare bedroom so I had to sleep on their living room floor, but it was better than being on the streets where many people end up after they have suffered tragedy in their lives.

It was not long before I was noticed that the council had found a local flat for me, so thankfully that ended my homeless experience. If anyone is ever in such a desperate situation, I would suggest that they seek guidance from housing charities or their local council.

I was fortunate to be able to draw a line in the sand as to my homeless situation, but there are many people who never find such help and end up on the streets where it becomes difficult to escape from. Whenever I see people sleeping in doorways and cardboard boxes, I remember my time of being homelessness and thank God that my situation was only temporary!

CHAPTER 10

My first unfoldment

A t the time of my first unfoldment, my ancestors (which included my grandmother) visited me in a spirit dream as they wanted me to understand what had occurred in the past, so that history did not repeat itself. In that dream, I was told by my ancestors that they believed they had 'influence' over people, and that they felt guilty that people would give them things because they loved them. They told me that the family was allowed to earn a living, but they must not take advantage of the influence that they believed they had. After considering what I was told in this spirit dream I believe that my ancestors misunderstood their gifts!

My grandmother told me that when I was a child, I might have thought that she did not love me. She made it clear to me that this was not the case and explained that the reason she found it hard to look at me was because my light was so bright. She told me that people would be drawn to me like a moth to a candle when they were crying out for help, and that this was a family trait. I knew this was true because people had frequently told me about my light throughout my journey! It took me a while before I understood what my grandmother meant by 'influence', but I did recognise that people were being drawn to me!

After this dream, my first unfoldment began. I started experiencing strange occurrences, like spirit writing all night, seeing light coming from my hands in a mirror in a dark room and seeing my grandmother's face transfigure over mine. My grandmother had also warned me that I would be seeing spirit soon, and not to be scared. She also directed me to Sutton Spiritualist Church for guidance.

It was at this church where I experienced a table tilting incident, where a table rose into the air and my grandmother spoke to me clearly for the first time. It was the first time that I became aware of spirit energy around me, and from that moment I knew that everything that had been foretold to me in my spirit dream was true, and that my life was changing beyond all recognition.

I was so happy that my dreams had turned into reality, but I was sad because I knew that my life would never be the same again. I felt like a chrysalis before it opens out into a butterfly. I knew the future would be amazing, but I did not know what was going to happen, just like a butterly does not know what is going to happen to it – it just accepts!

By asking for spirit's help in a difficult time of my life, I had accepted spirit into my life, and there was no way of going back. This was now who I was. I realised that there was a risk that the world might not understand what I was telling them, but I knew that it was part of my journey to use my abilities to help others with theirs, so I had to forget about any fear that I had and move forwards into the bright sunlight, sharing my knowledge with anyone and everyone who would listen to me!

Using my 'inner knowing' mediumship, I understood that years ago people were not so knowledgeable about spiritual matters, and what my ancestors had feared was not 'influence' but 'mediumship'. They had been open to spirit all the time, which is why they were perceived as being 'good people'. Their spiritual light had shone onto the world, like mine did, drawing people in need to them, just like my grandmother told me that I would. I now believe that it was this light which had been recognised by the senior partner when I was pregnant!

My ancestors' lack of knowledge had caused misunderstandings and misconceptions going back generations. So, in essence, not knowing about a 'gift' can be worse than 'knowing' because if you know at least you can learn how to use that gift.

In trying to unravel the truth, I discovered that some members of the family had not been told of their abilities, which had caused them problems throughout their lives. I came to this conclusion after being told by one of my uncles (whilst he was alive) that my mother was one of the family members who was not told, and she had experienced problems throughout her life because she was not able to use her gift to protect herself.

I am sure that my grandmother would not have deliberately caused her children to have the wrong information.

I believe that in my grandmother's day people did not understand enough about mediumship, so this had caused issues going back generations. This is a clear example of how lack of information can cause problems!

Even from a young age, I had felt a presence from my mother's side of the family. I now understood that it was this presence that made them fearful they were influencing people, when in fact they were just open to spirit, which was attracting people to them. My ancestors feared this presence, just like I did when I first felt it. It was now clear to me that I had inherited this family presence, and it was this that had been felt by my work colleagues in the city which made them all love me.

When my last manager had been trying to help me, he discovered that I had made more of an impact in one year than he had done in five years! This amazed him and was one of the reasons why he tried to fight for my retention in that firm. Unfortunately, I was unable to tell the world clearly what was happening to me as I feared telling the truth. As a result, no-one was able to help me which lead to my losing my career in the legal profession.

I never believed for a second that my family's presence was bad, and that made me even more determined to discover the truth.

Fear can be a terrible thing. I wanted the fear to end, and to restore not just mine, but my family's name. What I clung onto was the fact that I knew my ancestors had been good people, along with the fact that 'no-one can influence anyone!' They were simply good people, who were attracting people to them for guidance, just like my grandmother told me about moths being drawn to a flame. I was so happy that I had unravelled my family misunderstanding as this enabled me to understand my path more clearly! The final message my ancestors told me was that I was the only one who could put matters right to help people understand spiritual matters and not to fear their unfoldment (development).

If my ancestors had not made me aware of my mediumistic abilities via my spirit dream 12 years ago, and had I not learnt how to use my ability, I would not have discovered my spiritual pathway. I would also not have unearthed the family mystery which had caused misunderstandings and disharmony within my mother's family going back generations.

One Arthur Findlay medium, during a spiritual assessment, told me that I was now "flying the flag for my family', and they had gathered around me to clear misunderstandings. People in the past were scared of experiencing spiritual phenomena, but now that time has passed, and they should no longer be scared!

CHAPTER 11

Erdington Christian Spiritualist Church

After another long search for answers, I was pleased to find Erdington Christian Spiritualist Church.

From the moment I walked into this little church, Linda Wilson walked over to me and hugged me, I felt truly loved. The love that I felt was not just from the members of this church, but also from spirit. This love was pure. It was breathtaking. Consequently, I started to go to this church regularly and I made many lovely friends. What I admired the most was that nobody complained if the mediums had a bad night there. All that was important was that the church was filled with the love of 'God'.

I started my spiritual journey reading spiritual texts at their Sunday services, and I quickly became aware that I was connecting to spirit when I was reading. Reading made me very happy, and I sang out the Lord's praises when I read spiritual passages.

At one service, Eddie Cullen (now deceased), who was

an experienced medium, was inspired when I read a passage and he said out aloud that the Lord would be using my voice soon. Years later, I now know that he was right, and here I am writing this book, using my voice to help people realise that spirit guidance is there if you need it! Remember, we all have free will, so it is up to us whether we accept any spirit guidance that we receive.

After attending Erdington Christian Spiritualist Church for a while, I discovered their Pilgrim's Progress Workshop Spiritualist Course, which was a spiritual enlightenment course. I would suggest that if you are considering whether a spiritual course is suitable that you perhaps talk to members of the church who have completed the course to see whether it is suitable for you. I later became aware that it is not always clear what spiritual courses entail.

From the moment I was asked to stand on the rostrum, I could not believe how good I felt, sharing my life experiences with the congregation. I finally felt that I was putting my life experiences to good use. I also felt that this was a healing experience for me. I was elated that people listened to me and valued what I said. I now believe that spirit had led me into the city to build up my skillset so that I could help others. Spirit knew what a good communicator I was, and wanted me to put my gifts to good use.

I progressed well on their Pilgrims Progress Course, and I soon became aware that my 'hands' were 'my thing'. Consequently, I became proficient in ribbon reading, which was witnessed by the congregation on various occasions. As soon as I picked the ribbons up, I could feel the energy flowing through my fingers.

The best link that I did was for a man, who had been a medium the whole of his life, and he told me that he had never experienced anyone using ribbons the way I did! I was a bit scared when I gave this reading because I blacked out when I gave this message. I was an inexperienced medium at this time, and this experience surprised and shocked me. After talking to experienced mediums since, it appears that this is a normal experience. This experience did, however, provide me with further evidence of how spirit was working with me. Unfortunately, however, when the church asked me to drop the ribbons to give links, I could not do it as I had become 'deeply' attached to them.

What I did not understand at this time, was that I was struggling to make links to spirit on the rostrum without my ribbons. I was aware that I was seeing spirit, but I did not realise the importance of 'talking' to spirit. I now understand that it is important to remember that spirits are still people who want to communicate, so it is important to talk to them. It would take many years before I could work without the ribbons. The man that I gave this reading to said it would be 8 years. He explained that the spirit world do not have any concept of time like us!

Although I had enjoyed my time at Erdington Church and gained very valuable skills, I felt a yearning to progress with my knowledge. I strongly believe that spirit at this time inspired me to do a degree to help me understand and improve my communication skills. I was once again doing things 'for a purpose' - something one manager had made me aware of in the past.

Unfortunately, when I tried to return to Erdington Church, after I finished my degree 5 years later, it was at the time of Covid-19, and they were struggling to keep their doors open. My little church, in my absence, had been going downhill. My only option now was to return to Sutton Coldfield Spiritualist Church after a long period away. If I had not trusted my feelings to return there, I would have lost the chance to meet some lovely people and begin my journey properly, with love in my heart once more!

Erdington Church has now transformed into Ray Wilson Healing Sanctuary, details of which are in the Bibliography at the back of this book.

* * *

CHAPTER 12

Sensing grief for first time

I did not understand the pain of death until I lost my parents. First, my father, then my mother. One by one, my relatives were passing away. As each one passed, I became aware that my messages first came from my grandmother, then my father, and then my mother, in that order - not just to me but also through other mediums. Even though I now believed in my spirit messages, I had developed a habit of constantly checking my messages against other medium's messages, a habit which I still have not broken away from!

There were many times in my life when I had not got on well with my mother, but since her passing, I now believe that I can hear her clearer than ever. She was finally talking and not shouting at me, and because of this I was now listening to every word she said to me. When I was a child, she would shout and strut her stuff in front of me like a peacock, but now she came through with 'love' and I 'listened'. Of course, I always knew that she did love me, but her shouting made me recoil into my shell, and I developed a flight response whenever she shouted at me, which is the same as animals do when they feel that they are in danger.

From listening to my experiences, I am sure that any parents amongst you can recognise that it is important for them to be careful, not only with what they say to their children, but also in the way they say it, as harsh words can impact on your child's confidence, which can affect their whole life. It is important to try and stop mistakes and misunderstandings before they happen, as they might be hard to rectify years later.

From the many messages that came through for me from my parents, through mediums, it was obvious that they realised that they had made mistakes with me, and it was clear that they were trying their utmost to put things right. Whilst attending a séance for the first time (performed by a well-known medium) my mother spoke about how she was proud of me, and how much she loved me, but she did wish she could have supported me through 'difficult times'. In reply, I told her that she did help me in the end, and that is what mattered. I was so happy to hear my mother's voice again - not the overbearing mother that used to shout who I did not listen to, but a more compassionate mother. As a result of this message, and many others which came through various mediums, I received a constant stream of love and guidance which subsequently helped me with my grief and my understanding of my own journey.

Some people are worried that if they ask their friends

and relatives in spirit for messages that they will be causing them harm. This is not true, they are just as relieved to talk to you again as you are to talk to them. Allowing them to come through to say sorry gives them relief which will allow them to progress in the Spirit World, should they wish to.

My belief in the afterlife grew even more after receiving all the lovely messages from my parents and my grandparents. I always believed that my mother would be the one in charge, and I was right. My grandmother rarely came through after the death of my parents, which proved to me that the reins had been handed over to my mother.

Now that I believe in my spirit messages, I am now able to communicate freely with my family whenever I wish - mainly my mother. It is like they are still 'alive', only better. My mother now spoke to me from the heart in a way that she never did in her lifetime, and this has made me love her in a different way, more than I ever did before!

If you want to hear your relatives in the Spirit World, I advise you visit a local Spiritualist Church and when you attend make sure that you 'listen' to messages that come through. I would suggest that if you wish to receive messages from your relatives that you give them permission to come through, as they do need your permission! It is also useful to note these messages down (if this is not done by a scribe during services) so that you can make sense of them later.

Another way of communicating with your relatives is by listening to your dreams, as spirit will frequently try to use your dreams to communicate, which was how spirit liked to communicate with myself. I would suggest that you think of a question before you go to bed, and wait to see if you get a reply from your ancestors. If they want you to remember the message, you will!

I am now aware that there is no need to grieve as our loved ones are around us, . Everyone, even if they are not a medium is able to communicate with their loved ones!

Love binds us all in this world and the next!

CHAPTER 13

My second unfoldment

The reason I did not complete my development at my first unfoldment was because I became too scared to proceed, and I did not know who to approach for help. I was also coping with my marriage break-up at the time, so I decided to shut spirit communication down.

The fear that I felt during this period was the exact same fear that I used to feel when I was working in the city alongside people I did not feel at ease with. Despite shutting down to spirit for some time, I was aware that they were still trying to assist me by sending various people my way to help me believe in myself and my abilities again. One lesson that I learnt from my first unfoldment was that it is one thing being aware of an ability and another thing knowing how to use it. It is for this reason that I believe I was directed to return to Sutton Cold!eld Spiritualist Church so that I could proceed with my training.

My second unfoldment was sparked when I had the

time to devote to my spiritual development, after the death of my parents, as I was no longer tied by Earthly shackles. At this time I not only believed in my abilities, but I had the means to continue, due to the hard work of my parents during their lifetime. On my return to Sutton Coldfield Spiritualist Church, it was clear to me that the atmosphere had changed. It now seemed more welcoming and inviting. I was of course now more receptive to spiritual life with a more positive outlook, so this could be the reason why I felt the atmosphere more inviting.

After six weeks of visiting Sutton Cold!eld Spiritualist Church, to my surprise, I received messages from my parents via various mediums every week for six weeks. No-one knew my story there, so I believe that my messages were genuine. This surprised me as, when I had attended 12 years previously, I never used to get any messages, but this could have been that I was not aware of any loved ones in spirit at the time - this does not mean that there was not any though, just that I was not aware of any!

These messages mainly consisted of my parents apologising and giving me encouragement that they would back me with whatever I wanted to do with my life. My grandparents also came through with similar messages. These messages were just what I needed to reassure me that I had my ancestors' blessings to being a medium. This approval had been playing on my mind since my spirit dream 12 years before when I was warned to only use my ability for good!

During my time with this church, I discovered some amazing workshops and regularly attended anything that was available to improve my spiritual knowledge. However, what I needed most was to develop further as a medium and to learn how to use my mediumistic skill to the best of my ability. Consequently, I decided to join mediumship training with Jean Kelford and Chris Beech, who are both international mediums. I soon learnt that this class was all about linking to spirit in preparation to work on the rostrum. I knew that I had to try to forget what I had learnt in the past and learn how to link the SNU way.

In between my mediumistic training, I continued to go to their Sunday services at this church. One service that I will never forget was when Jacqui Rogers (a well-known medium who could see auras) was the visiting medium. As usual, I sat on the front row, hoping for a message, just the same as everyone else. She immediately homed in on me, telling me how strong my light was. In her words: 'Your light is filling this church. You are amazing!' She then asked, 'Are you a soldier for God?' and I had to admit that I was. If I had said 'No', I would have been turning God away, and I did not want to do this. Her words filled me with love and encouragement. I was overjoyed that someone had finally recognised me for who I was. Someone had seen and recognised my light, just like my grandmother had told me at my first unfoldment. In her words, she had given me the key to my door, which she said was the most that any medium could do. She said that you can give people the key to their door, but you could not make them go through the door!

I continued with my mediumistic training, which

went from strength to strength, and as the weeks passed, I gained more and more friends at this church. I enjoyed sharing stories with people who had obviously had similar experiences to myself.

As my spiritual knowledge grew, I gained a deeper understanding of the meaning of spiritual philosophy, which is the basis of the religion of spiritualism. Subsequently, I became aware that spirit was directing me to do a healing course to mend fences from the past, and to enable me to move forwards.

CHAPTER 14

Need to heal

When I realised that I had hit a barrier with my development and wondered what was holding me back, I concluded that I needed to heal. I knew that I had to get rid of the fear of my development and hurt which I had been holding onto from my past. I realised that it was important to get rid of Earthly baggage to make way for my spiritual awakening.

To bring healing into your life, and to invite a spiritual awakening, it is important to focus on your end goal of being healed and what might be getting in the way of that healing. I would suggest that it helps to write these down in a journal and to start to work towards that end goal. The first thing that you need to do, to invite a spiritual awakening to transform your life, is declutter to get rid of barriers. It is necessary for you to declutter both your physical and spiritual self to make room for the new you. You need to clear your space of the stuff that you no longer need which serves as a distraction from your life. Decluttering your physical space is a start. Then it is important to declutter your mind. To do this, take time every day to sit in silence and solitude. Allow your thoughts to pass without judgment and slowly watch your mind clear of mental clutter. Meditation allows you to relax and offers you a greater connection to your intuition which is your spiritual guidance.

Once you have decluttered, it is important to examine your beliefs and be conscious of what you believe. It is important to understand the energy that you are putting out, not only into your world, but into the world at large. It is important to be honest when you consider whether your beliefs are supporting your spiritual growth. Sometimes a spiritual awakening requires letting go of beliefs we have held for most of our entire lives. When considering moving forward to a spiritual awakening, you must first realise that you have been sleeping.

After examining your beliefs, it is important to expand your mind, expand new ideas and differing beliefs. For this, you should read books and attend lectures and have conversations with people who have lived different lives for guidance. An awakening occurs when you have learned something new, when you have 'quite literally' woken your mind, and your spirit awakens from a slumber you perhaps didn't even know you were in. When you expand your mind to allow in new ideas, beliefs, and possibilities, you increase the opportunity to wake up to a life experience you never knew was possible.

After expanding your mind, the next stage is to go outside. There is energy, spirit and magic in the outdoors. So many of us spend our time cooped up inside, sitting behind computer screens, not truly connected to the world (or to ourselves). It is important to take time to connect with nature. Even in the big cities you can find trees to touch, gardens to admire, fresh air to breathe. Try not to distract yourself with your phone, or even another person's company. Give yourself the quiet and the solitude and the presence that comes with being outside. You may be surprised by what comes alive within you!

On your healing journey it is also important to take care of yourself by eating healthily and staying active, which are great ways to stay connected to yourself and your 'higher power'. As soon as you have dealt with issues inside and outside your body, you will be in a better position to move forward with your spiritual awakening and your spiritual journey. Do not be afraid to ask for guidance on your spiritual journey from your local Spiritualist Church, and your Spirit Guides who are always there with you, even if you are not aware that they are!

Years ago I was told that I was a healer, but I did not take this seriously because I did not understand the true meaning of '*healing*'. By the time of my second unfoldment, I felt a yearning to begin my healing journey. I was surprised to find how easy came to me once I recognised that healing was the most important part of my journey.

My friends at Sutton Church noticed a change in me, and I noticed a change in myself. Every time I performed healing, I felt that healing was being given to myself. As my spiritual attunement grew, I gained a greater under-standing of the true meaning of the second principle, 'Brotherhood of Man'.

CHAPTER 15

Predictions

I will now talk about what made me come to the realisation that I was a psychic medium, and that I was connecting to spirit for answers. As my life unfolded, I recognised that I had experienced many visions and received many messages which later became reality. So, the moral of this story is to listen to your inner voice just in case spirit are trying to direct you with your life journey, which is what happened to me!

At the time of my awakening, I finally came to the conclusion that that spirit was making me remember my life journey to help me understand my unfoldment so that I could help others with theirs!

MY PREDICTIONS

As a child, I was told in a dream the name of the man that I would marry and that he would treat me badly.

Because I was so young when I had this dream, I never paid attention to it. This prediction came true.

Whilst working at various solicitors' offices in the city, I used to regularly experience gut instincts about problems within such firms. .As time passed and I moved from job to job, all my predictions came true one by one.

In a dream, years before the event, I saw myself in a hotel room where my parents visited me. This prediction came true at the time of my marriage breakdown.

In a spirit dream, I saw myself in a journalist's office, trying to get them interested in a story that I had to tell. I did not understand this vision at the time. I told them that I wanted my story o be published in their newspaper. Of course, they did not listen to what I said. They only wanted an advert from me to advertise my psychic services after I had told them that I was a psychic medium. Although the meaning of this dream did not make sense to me at the time, it later occurred to me that I was being prepared to give them a story in the future.

Whilst at the last firm that I worked for, I sent in various sick notes. On one sick note that I sent in, for some reason I scribbled that I was going to write a famous book just like J. K. Rowling did with the Harry Potter books. I now believe that I was making the prediction that I was going to write my first book, which is what you are reading now!

At the time of my first unfoldment, my manager said that I did everything for a 'purpose'. I believe that it appeared that I was doing everything for a purpose because I was predicting what was going to happen in the future.

In conclusion, I now believe that all my life spirit had been preparing me with the necessary life skills so that I could share my knowledge of unfoldment with the world! All I wanted to do was to help people understand their own inner spirit so that they could share this with others!

CHAPTER 16

Strange occurrences

A s my strange occurrences grew throughout my journey, I started to document them. The reason I did this was because at times even I wondered whether I was imagining it all! I did not realise until years later that I had been documenting my experiences so that one day I could write this book!

I have put these occurrences in approximate date order, so that you can see how they progressed throughout my life and increased with intensity at the time of my first and second unfoldment when I finally concluded that I was a psychic medium. Every experience that I had gave me the confidence to move forward, to believe in myself, and to recognise that my beliefs and abilities were not all in my head!

OCCURRENCES

Whilst on a holiday with family to Cornwall at a

young age, I went out to sea with my father in a small dinghy, the sea was like a mill pond, no sign of waves. A huge wave came from nowhere and I remember that I blanked out when I plunged into the water. The next thing that I remember is being dragged out of the sea by my father who was desperately trying to save me. I will never forget what it felt like. I emerged gasping for air, feeling the pressure of the water around my body. My father had been frantically diving trying to find me amongst the waves. When he found me, he lifted me up with his strong arms, lifting me up into the air.

My father (in spirit) years later came back to remind me about this incident and he told me that he would always be with me to hold me up in difficult times. I believe this was a near-death experience which I never forgot.

What interests me is how I blacked out at the time I entered the water. I believe this is what happens when we are approaching death and spirit comes to grab us to take us to the Spirit World. I have read many accounts of people around the world who report similar near-death experiences.

During a shorthand incident at college, when I read out a passage to the class in a strange tongue, no-one said anything to me, and the class continued as if nothing had happened. No one questioned my behaviour either. I still don't understand the significance of this. It was obviously the start of my spiritual life, as this was the first of many spiritual experiences that I had!

Whilst taking three-hour exams at college, and whilst I

was studying for my degree, I became aware that during exams I would go blank, and when I came around the exam was over. During one law exam, I finished an hour early and still got a top mark – all without any memory of what I had written! I now believe that my exam experiences were my doing and that somehow, I had learned how to go into a trance. I do not believe these occurrences were spirit-led as I don't believe they would have been allowed to do this. Spirit was giving me the confidence to take these exams by helping me use the information which had been in my head all my life. I have recently been told by an experienced medium that spirit can do this!

I had a spirit dream, which happened at the start of my first unfoldment, when my grandmother and descendants visited me to guide me on my marriage breakdown, and to make me aware of my spiritual abilities. I can remember this spirit dream, which was 12 years ago, as if it was yesterday. It is my belief that spirit dreams are usually prophetic. Normal dreams are quickly forgotten, but spirit dreams are remembered.

It is a good idea to have a notebook and pen by your bedside to make notes of anything what you consider is important in your dreams as most people can't remember their dream when they wake up.

At the time of my first unfoldment, I was aware of my close connection to my grandmother. I became aware that she was encouraging me to do things like stand in front of a large mirror to prepare me for working on the church rostrum, and she overshadowed my face with hers in a bathroom mirror which is called *'transfiguration'*. She also encouraged me to go to Sutton Church where I witnessed her communicating to me through a raised table for the first time. This is called 'table tilting'.

As the table raised, I felt her energy come through. This was the strongest spirit energy I had ever felt. It was like she was standing by my side. I also was aware that she was talking to me telepathically.

Whilst trying to understand my dissatisfaction with being a legal secretary, I could not fathom why I was never happy and kept moving from one firm to another. I now realise that spirit was showing me that I was capable of so much more and that is why I was unhappy.

Whilst I was on the operating table at Good Hope Hospital, undergoing a C-section, giving birth to my son, I lost a lot of blood. I believe this was another near-death experience. I remember saying in my mind that I would give my life for my son, but I was subsequently told that it was not my time!

There is one significant incident that I can remember, whilst working for a large solicitors in the city whilst I was pregnant, the senior partner approached me and put his hands on my tummy and said, 'Bless you.' I believe he saw my light, just as my grandmother told me about in my spirit dream. Jacqui Rogers also referred to my light when she first saw me on the front row of a Sunday congregation at Sutton Coldfield Spiritualist Church. I also believe that people who I worked with throughout my career also saw my light, which is why my work colleagues loved me. One which one lady subsequently came back to tell me years later through a medium to tell me how much she respected me as a work colleague.

Whilst working for a firm of solicitors in Sutton Cold-field, my manager told me to write down all my concerns. When he considered everything that I had written, he said he could see that I seemed to be doing everything for a purpose, and that something was going on, but he did not have time to go through all of it. Consequently, I had to leave this firm as I just couldn't concentrate on my work anymore as I was too focused on having a spiritual life.

Whilst visiting a coffee shop at the time of my first unfoldment, when I was struggling to cope with my psychic ability, a tramp entered the shop begging for money. When he approached me, I could feel his pain. I took my purse out of my handbag and gave him the contents, which of course he was grateful for.

During the breakdown of my marriage, whilst I was still at my matrimonial home, pipes burst around the house, which could possibly have been poltergeist activity. The activity started whilst I was there, but increased with velocity after I had left.

I was aware of the continuance of the plumbing issues after I left as my ex-husband had posted on Facebook what was happening whilst he was there with our son. It was obvious that the whole house was in total devastation before he left! I have included a chapter on ghosts and poltergeist activity in Chapter 23.

As my development progressed, I noticed that strange people came up to me for guidance in the most unusual of places. One was at the local job centre, when a young man sat by my side, and asked me for my opinion on his troubled life. I took him to a local coffee shop to talk about his issues. The man was very apologetic about having to share his problems with me. The second was in a McDonald's toilet in Birmingham where I heard a woman crying out that her man had treated her badly and she asked for my guidance. My grandmother (in spirit) had told me that I was like a candle and that strangers would be drawn to my light for guidance, and this was exactly what was happening here!

Since the time of my first unfoldment, I also became aware that spirit was sending various people to me who all seemed to be making me aware of my abilities. One incident was where an established medium put two crosses in my hands. I made an immediate psychometric connection to his mum and dad. He said that he had never made a connection to his father before. I saw his dad as a grumpy old man, poking at his fire in desperation for it to work. I also saw his mother as a ballerina. He confirmed that everything I said was correct! I believe this was spirit trying to show me that I had the ability of psychometry and it again proved that my abilities were intensifying. I also recognised that when I was more relaxed, my abilities were stronger.

Spirit inspired me to do a degree, the purpose of which was to improve my communication skills so that I could understand my own unfoldment and be able to help others with theirs. I believe that spirit helped me use the information in my mind to help me fulfil a deep desire which I had within me of achieving a degree. Although spirit was trying to help me, I believe they also had their own agenda in that they wanted me to use my knowledge to help others.

Throughout the time of my development, I became aware that spirit was using my keyboard skills, which I had gained as a legal secretary, to help me communicate with the outside world which I previously had issues with.

These are just a few of the many strange occurrences that have happened to me throughout the whole of my life. When I finally believed in my messages and my visions, it became obvious to me that spirit was making me remember the whole of my life for a 'purpose' which ties in with what one of my managers had said to me in the past!

Spirit came to me only when I asked them for help with my life. They will only come to you if you give your consent to help you!

CHAPTER 17

Hearing and believing

After documenting numerous strange occurrences and spirit messages throughout my life, I could no longer deny their existence. I believe that I documented these because I needed to prove, not just for others, but also to myself, what I had been experiencing over time.

One thing I was sure of was that whenever I believed in myself, good things happened, and when I did not believe in myself, bad things happened. I also became aware that when I started to believe in my abilities that they heightened. However, it did take me a while to find the right teacher though! My grandmother (in spirit) had taught me the basics of mediumship, but she did not teach me everything, as there is more information available now in the world than was available in her day! My teacher at Sutton Church told me that I had been held back due to my life experiences, which was certainly true!

On my journey, I came across barriers such as being

unable to talk about what I was experiencing because I was so scared, and when I was eventually able to talk about what had happened, I was still fearful that people would not believe me. I also came across barriers put up by other people and found it extremely difficult to find people who I trusted to get further guidance on my journey. However, as soon as I discovered Sutton Coldfield Spiritualist Church, which is connected to the Spiritualists'' National Union (SNU), I knew I was in good hands. I would urge my readers that if they are ever fearful of anything spiritual in their life that they should seek the guidance of their local Spiritualist Church who have experience of spiritual matters.

Now that I have finally told the people that matter about my spiritual journey, I am now free of barriers and ready to move forward on my correct spiritual path which was always intended for me!

I sincerely hope that you discover the love of spirit and that you learn to trust in your Spirit Guides, as I did, so that they can guide you whenever you need their help!

CHAPTER 18

Spirituality and Spiritualism

On my journey, I learned that these two terms are often misunderstood. Although both words look alike, their meanings are very different from each other. I shall therefore examine each of them in detail.

SPIRITUALITY

Spirituality exists within the mind of a person. It is a condition or a state that is achieved by a person, maybe after a long period of attempts and trials e.g., yoga, acupuncture. It is a state of mind that is achieved based on a subjective experience or according to religious ideals. In similar terms, we can identify 'spirituality' in people who have attained an extreme state of mind, which is far more beyond the physical existence. This can also be identified as a process of human transformation from one psychological state to another. Many religions have identified this psychological transformation of the mind and have interpreted it in many ways. However, spirituality is not a product of religion only, but the person who should put his/her effort in achieving the state of mind or the higher level. Spirituality does not have a direct relationship with the outer appearance of the person, and he/she may remain like the same, but his/her inner self is much more advanced.

SPIRITUALISM

Spiritualism, however, is a religious and people who follow this religion believe that the spirit of a dead person can communicate with the living. People who follow this religion call themselves 'Spiritualists'. The spirit comes through the medium, whoever that may be, with the desire of passing on love and encouragement. Spiritualists either communicate with spirit themselves or visit establishments where they ask mediums to allow their loved ones to come through with messages for them. They might either ask for a private reading or visit a church, and within their mind ask for their loved ones to come through. There is no exact science to this. If the enquirer does not receive any messages from a medium, it might be for any number of reasons. What happens frequently is that the sitter wants a certain spirit to come through, but instead another spirit comes through, which may be because that spirit believes that his message has greater priority.

Spiritualists believe that, when a person dies, he/she has an afterlife and can keep in contact with the living.

However, this has many interpretations in different religions. Some of the things that are commonly shared by all the believers of spiritualism include their belief that the soul of a person exists in an afterlife, These afterlife beings are usually called 'spirits' and they are believed to be able to communicate with living people.

The world of spirit is not a static or a stable place, as spirits can evolve should they so wish. It is also possible for them to rebirth. Moreover, spiritualists believe that spirit provides knowledge on God and the afterlife, too. There are many followers of spiritualism around the world and many people are attracted to this religion because it does not tie them to any religious texts like other religions and that they have a chance to put rights wrongs in their life in the hear and now.

SIMILARITIES

Considering the similarities between the two terms, we can see that both have a connection with the idea of an existence that is beyond the human faculty. Also, both these terms have their own religious interpretations. In terms of the difference, 'spiritualism' is achieved by somebody after his/her death, whereas 'spirituality' 'is a state of mind which is achieved within the human life itself.

WHAT DOES SPIRITUALISM OFFER AS A RELIGION?

Spiritualism is too diverse to have a universal code of

beliefs. Instead, spiritualists accept a set of more wider ranging principles'. Baker, President of the Havant Spiritualist Church says that:

'Spiritualists believe in freedom of religion and freedom of worship and that you worship God in your own way. Spiritualism gives you a set of values that enables you to think about how your relationship with God should be'.

The UK and the USA have their own version of these principles surrounding the Philosophy of Spiritualism.

SNU's SEVEN PRINCIPLES (UK)

The Spiritualists' National Union (n.d) (SNU) in the UK, bases itself on the Seven Principles, which all full members must accept.

- The first of these principles relates to accepting God as the creative force in the Universe, and that they are part of the life created by God.
- The second of these principles relates to human beings being members of one divine family because they are from the same creative force. It is important to understand the needs of other individuals to assist them, not only to the material necessities of their fellow creatures, but also to their spiritual needs.
- The third of these principles relates to spiritualists believing that communication with departed spirits occurs. Their churches provide venues where communication,

through mediumship, is possible and many deceased relatives and friends take advantage of this opportunity to continue to take an interest in the welfare of the living.

- The fourth of these principles refers to their belief in the continued existence of the human soul and states that matter (being part of the creative force, or energy) cannot be destroyed; it merely changes its form and that spirit, as it is part of the creative force, is therefore indestructible. When we die, our spirit becomes an integral part of the Spirit World. The Spirit World interpenetrates this material world, but in a different dimension. In spirit life, we have a spirit body, which until we progress far enough, is a replica of our Earthly body. Individuals in the Spirit World remain the same individuals with the same personalities and characteristics, and only progress through their own efforts. Individual personal responsibilities do not stop at death.

- The fifth principle relates to personal responsibility, and states that everyone is responsible for their wrongful thoughts and deeds. No other person or outside influence can interfere with an individual's spiritual development unless they allow them to.

- The sixth principle refers to the compensation and retribution hereafter for all the good and evil deeds done on Earth. *As you sow, so shall you reap*. These effects of this Law operate now, and you do not wait until life in the Spirit World.

- The seventh and final principle refers to the external progress that is open to every human soul. Every human spirit has the power to progress in wisdom and love. The rate of progress is directly proportional to the desire for mental and spiritual understanding. Each spirit can reform and deal with the wrong things it has done in the past.

THE NATIONAL ASSOCIATION OF SPIRITUALIST CHURCHES (USA) – NINE PRINCIPLES

The National Association of Spiritualist Churches (2016-2022) (USA) has nine principles, which provide more information about spiritualist beliefs. They believe in *infinite intelligence,* that the phenomena of nature, both physical and spiritual, are the expression of *infinite intelligence*. They affirm that a correct understanding of such expression and living in accordance therewith, constitute true religion. They affirm that the existence and personal identity of the individual continue after the change called *'death'*. They affirm that communication with the so-called dead is a fact, scientifically proven by the phenomena of spiritualism. They believe that the highest morality is contained in the Golden Rule:

'Do unto others as you would have them do unto you'. They affirm the moral responsibility of individuals, and that we make our own happiness or unhappiness as we obey or disobey nature's physical and spiritual laws.'

They affirm that the doorway to reformation is never closed against any soul here or hereafter. They affirm that the precepts of prophecy and healing are divine attributes proven through mediumship.

Spiritualism, in essence, encourages people to discover their own spiritual journey based on certain principles. It does not tie anyone down to any creeds or dogmas which many religions have. I believe that it is for this reason that many people are branching away from traditional religions that tie them to religious texts. This is what attracted me to spiritualism, because it encourages you to consider your own spiritual path based around certain principles and is not tied down to any religious texts!

CHAPTER 19

Spiritual development

W hen considering your own spiritual development beyond the physical existence, you cannot go far wrong by considering the words of mystics.

Sadhguru (2012) is dedicated to the physical, mental, and spiritual well-being of humanity. He possesses a perspective on life and living that never fails to intrigue, challenge, and surprise all he encounters. He regularly gives spiritual guidance on YouTube and one of these is 'Dimension Beyond the Physical' where he talks about development beyond our five senses.

In this YouTube clip, he talks about our physical body which has five senses which are sight, sound, smell, taste, and touch, which receives sensory information using these senses. To experience a dimension beyond the physical body, a perception beyond these senses must be developed or opened. These five senses work naturally for one's survival, and to go beyond these five senses we must strive to go beyond this barrier and develop perception beyond these senses. Your five senses naturally open the moment you leave your mother's womb because they are needed for survival. If you did not have them, you would not know how to survive. An example is where a child who is lost in the jungle who has found something edible to eat. They would naturally know to put it in their mouth. Nobody taught them this. Nobody instructed them on the way to eat. The natural skills such as eating, and walking are necessary for your survival, and you do not need any training as they are inbuilt. These inbuilt skills which are needed for survival open naturally without any striving.

There are other abilities that you are not aware of until you strive to achieve which include the abilities of being able to read and write. The way of developing perception beyond your 5 senses is known as "opening up" or "unfoldment".

All your sense organs are outward bound, you can see what is around you, but everything that you "experience" happens within you. You hear and see within you. You can see the whole world within you. An example is when you touch your friend's hand, you don't feel his hand, you can only feel your sensations on your hand. Everything that has happened to you, your joy and misery are within you – everything happens within you.

To develop your inner self and to look within you, you need to strive to achieve. Everything that we have is outward bound, but everything that is happening is within, so it gives you a false perception of what it is. To experience anything within you, you will have to strive for and develop. turning within ourselves, but this will require development training. "Spiritual development" is development beyond man's normal five senses which can be achieved by becoming more aware of yourself inwardly and of your surroundings. It is important to become aware of your own spiritual path to understand your development.

I conclude by saying that if you wish to develop beyond your five senses, the first step is to read spiritual books and attend circles and workshops at your local Spiritualist Church. You will discover that by mixing with likeminded people at such events you will be free to discuss any concerns that you might have in your development, and this will also help your understanding. Developing is individual and subjective, that is why it is important to discuss your journey with like-minded people who have had similar experiences without fear of reprisal!

CHAPTER 20

Near-death experiences

To consider near death experiences, it is necessary to consider the similarities between accounts of various people. I will let spirit have the last word on this subject by considering some of the messages from spirit which came through the mediumship of Leslie Flint (deceased).

There are many accounts of people from many different types of background around the world who have had 'near-death' experiences. I will now consider the account of a doctor who returned from a 'near-death' experience.

100huntley (2020) Dr Mark McDonough attended an interview, which was aired on YouTube on the 20th of April 2020. He wanted to share his 'near-death' experience to inspire others who had gone through similar tragedies. Unfortunately, he had suffered the tragedy of losing his mother and brother to a fire, where he tried to save them, but to no avail. At this time, he suffered multiple burns, and the pain he was suffering was so great that he asked God to take him. In his journey of recovery, he had to undergo multiple surgeries. He claims that the pain which he was experiencing was intense, but on seeing a white light he felt an awareness of 'love', his pain turned into a feeling of euphoria which took his pain away. During his surgery, he also claims that he was aware of being awake (even though he was not) and seeing his deceased relatives. He talks of a meeting between certain people, but he was not sure who they were. He was also told that it was not his time, and that he should return. Following on from this, he had more surgeries and was subsequently inspired by another doctor, whom he held in high regard. This doctor encouraged him to return to medical school to train as a trauma reconstructive surgeon. He says that he is sharing his story as he now wants to pass onto others the inspiration that he received at a difficult time of his life.

In considering the subjective accounts of various people, it is important to consider the similarities between them, despite their many and varied backgrounds. Similarities between these accounts include:

- Ability to know what is happening, not only around them, but beyond the room where they are – hearing/seeing/feeling their surroundings.
- Seeing a white light.

- Feeling unconditional love which took away their fear.
- Their pain leaves them, leaving them feeling euphoric.
- Feeling of becoming separate from their body.
- Feeling that they no longer must prove anything.
- Feeling of being loved, just because of their existence.
- Some are given the chance to remain in spirit or to return to Earth. If they choose to remain in spirit, they will be shown what effect this will have on their family. If they are encouraged to return from their near-death experience, they are given the message to return and to live life fearlessly!
- Meeting relatives.
- Acknowledging separability from everything else.
- Experiencing being in a realm where they do not feel tied by talking, as they feel the essence of people that are with them, communicating with their mind. They understand the situation they are in without talking. This suggests telepathic communication with spirits, which is what I have experienced myself.

In considering the many messages that came through Leslie Flint (medium) during his lifetime, they all have a similar message to pass on: they do not want us to fear death any longer. In their words

'There is no death, you return to a spiritual existence'.

In their many messages, they all claim to give us hope that there is survival after death, they talk about many things including what they experienced when they first entered the Spirit World. They talk about people retaining the same appearance and characteristics. They talk about life in the Spirit World. They talk about understanding the lower and higher realms, and their wish to inspire people that progression is available for all that seek it!

In conclusion, only subjective proof is available about life after death until science branches away from their requirement of 100% objective proof. However, one advancement that has been made by the medical profession is that they are now accepting a more holistic approach in treating physical illnesses, and now recognise inner conflicts and disharmonies as being the cause of many troubles which do not yield to normal physical medications. For this reason, it is now accepted by medical science that the human organism should be approached and treated with a far wider concept of its constitution. This is a significant breakthrough which means that the medical profession is now more tolerant of the connection between our physical and spiritual bodies which gives hope for their future acceptance of life after death!

* * *

CHAPTER 21

The Afterlife

The afterlife, also referred to as 'life after death' or 'the world to come', is a purported existence in which the essential part of an individual's identity, or their stream of consciousness, continues to live after the death of their physical body. We will now consider whether death is the end of consciousness or whether consciousness continues after death.

For spiritual people to consider that death is the end, is short-sighted. For scientists and the medical world to consider life after death without objective proof is an impossibility - until spirit convinces them, that is!

We will now consider various countries' beliefs on 'the continuous of the soul after death'. Many worldwide authors write about a trend towards people beginning to withdraw from certain religions and considering other directions such as 'spiritualism', due to them not wanting to be fearful of life after death anymore.

The five great world religions are Judaism, Christianity, Islam, Buddhism, and Hinduism, which all have their own unique sacred texts, and all believe in some version of a 'self', which mostly survives death.

Agnostics think that it is impossible to know whether there is a God or life after death.

Atheists believe that there is no God, and no life after death, and that death is the cessation of the existence of the individual.

Despite not believing in 'life after death', Agnostics and Atheists have reported having near-death experiences.

To consider what Atheists believe regarding life after death, we will now contemplate an excerpt from YouTube by NourFoundation (2014) discussing *Experiencing Death: An Insider's Perspective*. It focuses on the near-death experiences of Atheists and considers how much our prior beliefs shape our experiences. By considering two case studies, they question why Atheists have near-death experiences if they don't believe in angelic beings. The conclusion that they come to is:

'Just believing you don't believe anything is going to happen, does not stop it happening'.

The first case that they consider is that of a lady who was careful in her interpretation, but claimed that she *'dissolved into pure energy, and when she reached the light, she had an overwhelming experience of love'.*

The other case study involved someone who claimed they saw dead relatives, which is common in near-death experiences. The final decision that they came to was that *'just because you do not believe that something is going to happen does not stop it happening'.*

Other religions that do believe in life after death base their belief on teachings in their scriptures or traditions. But the religion of spiritualism not only believes in life after death, they also regularly demonstrate this by allowing spirits to come through mediums with messages from the afterlife.

Since the beginning of the internet, people have been searching for answers regarding whether there is an 'after life'. We will now consider a scientific view.

Farafan, A. (2017) claims that they can 'prove' that the soul does not 'DIE: It returns to the UNIVERSE'. This article was written by two scientists who question and tackle the age-old question:

'Is there life after death?'

Their theory is that when we die, the contents of 'micro- tubules' (as they call them) return to the universe. Although this account is interesting, it is clearly written by scientists, who only believe in science. They do not even consider that there may be spiritual answers to explain 'life after death', which appears to be shortsighted considering the many accounts available to the contrary.

Let's just say that their assumption of the human soul dissipating into the universe is true. How then can thousands of mediums be getting messages from different spirits, if a person's consciousness is 'dissipating' to a universal memory where everyone's energy becomes one? This just doesn't make sense! Remember, there are many mediums all over the world who truly believe they are connecting with the Spirit World, and we owe it to them to consider their opinions when considering whether there is 'life after death'. It could be argued that there is one universal mind. If this is the case why do some mediums claim they cannot link to some spirits, saying 'I do not know your relative!' If there was a universal mind surely they should be able to link to everyone if all consciousness becomes one!

Even the film world has embraced the World of Spirit by depicting people having contact with the Spirit World. Examples of these films include the *Sixth Sense*, *Beetlejuice*, *What Dreams May Come,* and *Ghost,* to name but a few.

We will now consider Spirit's last word on life after death. After listening to many accounts of The Leslie Flint Trust (1997-2022), spirits come back with their love and with the aim of proving the continuous existence of the human soul after death. They come to tell us what a beautiful, magical place the Spirit World is and how we keep the same characteristics that we have on Earth. They also tell us that it is up to us whether we wish to progress to higher realms where we no longer need to be recognised as we were on Earth.

'You are not in a dark room forever; it is the start of a great journey!'

CHAPTER 22

Spirit speaks through me

The following messages were sent by spirit through me, the first whilst I was in a trance state and the second whilst I was in a conscious state, whilst using a typewriter.

COPING WITH LONELINESS

The following message came through me to help a German lady who was suffering with loneliness. I attended a trance lesson at Arthur Findlay College on 4th October 2021, at which I was invited to connect to fellow students and practise trance mediumship. I connected to a German lady, who witnessed my trance state and made the following comments after.

She talked about how my message touched her as it gave her solace as to her loneliness. This was the first time that I had experienced induced trance mediumship.

She said that when I started, she could see a flickering

of my eyes. There was something behind me. It seemed to her like a halo.

She could also see some heat when I connected. She could see it rather than feel it.

There was a strong palpitation of my heat. Before and later, it slowed down.

There was a nice and strong energy around me. The blending was wonderful. It was a perfect match.

She said that my message really touched her because what I talked about was also her topic, when the world would come together as one.

The following are my exact words which she recorded.

'...Many people have many different thoughts. Many people only listen to their own thoughts. The understanding is not always easy. When there is understanding, there is happiness and no sadness. We should realise that we are not alone. They send love to us and words that are needed. When we are all aware, people will understand. The knowledge comes down to everyone who is ready to receive the knowledge. Some people may question spirit intelligence, but the knowledge only comes to those that are ready for it. Ask, and the true meaning of love will come to us, and then everyone will be together as one. We will be one voice, no separation of language. We will understand each other. When people work together and stand together, they will not stand apart, and everyone will share the love. Stop and listen. Stop and share.

The German lady said that what touched her the most was when I was referring to 'loneliness', as that was what she was experiencing at the time. She enjoyed hearing about the love that was there – the oneness and togetherness!

COPING WITH THE LOSS OF A LOVED ONE

The following spirit message was sent to help people cope with the loss of a loved one. I was fully conscious, using a typewriter, when this message came through me.

I am trying to share my love.
I am trying to share my memories.
You think you cannot hear me, but you can.
My words will not be words like you are used to, they will be like the sounds of a rustling tree, so listen carefully.
At first, my words will seem just like sounds, but relax and you will understand my message to you.
You think that I am far away, but I am closer than you think.
I am but a thought away whenever you need my support.
You wish you had said certain words to me before I passed.
Don't worry, I heard you speak those words to me in your thoughts.
I now feel what you felt, and see what you have seen, and what you see now.
I am here for you. I am Spirit. We are both Spirit.

I never know when spirit is going to send the next message. On a few occasions they have woken me up in the middle of the night when I can feel them drawing me to the keyboard. The feeling is so intense, they fill my mind with so much love it is hard not to do as they wish.

All they wish to do is to share their love with the world. All they wish to do is to help us not to be so scared of death and to value our time on the Earth plane and to learn about our spiritual journey, which is to not only to look after ourselves, but to look after each other, physically and spiritually.

* * *

CHAPTER 23

Spirit speaks on ghosts

L eslie Flint was a very powerful physical medium whose lifetime spanned from 1911 to 1994. His mediumship was unique because he connected to spirits via a voice box, which appeared above his head, through which spirit spoke.

The following is an account of a spirit message which came through Leslie from Harry Price, the well-known British psychical researcher and author.

Harry Price is best remembered for his investigations into the haunting of Borley Rectory in Essex. On 19th December 1963, Harry gave a detailed account, through Leslie, explaining the difference between ghosts and spirit.

This message is one of many that comes from Leslie's archives, which are now maintained by The Leslie Flint Trust (1997-2022). The following transcript of the recording of Harry Price is produced with their kind permission. In this recording, Harry Price talks about ghosts, which he studied when he was alive. He said that spirit believed mankind needed guidance on this subject.

You will notice that, as this is a message from Harry Price, it is in the first person. I have also put the discussion in italics.

HARRY PRICE (DECEASED) ON 'GHOSTS', COURTESY OF THE LESLIE FLINT TRUST (1997-2022) TRANSCRIPT

Harry Price: N*ow I am on the other side; I realise how difficult it is to prove anything appertaining to psychic matters in a purely material or scientific way. We must accept the fact that scientific proof – that is the kind of proof that would appeal and would be accepted, strictly on scientific grounds or scientific basis by scientific minds – is practically impossible to prove 100%. It may to some extent accept with reservations, but science is too anxious for 100% proof on a scientific basis of something which I feel cannot be accepted scientifically or proved scientifically. I come to give a talk on ghosts to answer certain problems about them.*

Often one hears of ghosts and entities that haunt a certain place, often for centuries, and sometimes they are, according to the mentality of the ghosts in question, a nuisance and sometimes they are very much undesirable from the point of view that they disturb and frighten individuals who happen to be living on the premises. Firstly, I should differentiate because there are varying kinds of ghosts.

First, you have the ghost of an individual, perhaps long

since dead, that has no connection with the actual spirit of the person concerned. You may have a very powerful thought force which may, by its very power, give the impression that the individual person or personality is there at the haunting. There are a lot of people, when they have seen what they term to be a ghost, are under the impression that they are seeing the apparition in outward shape and form of the individual who has long since been dead. What is happening there is that the individual concerned is not necessarily present. This is an astral projection upon the atmosphere which on certain occasions (usually because the atmosphere is conducive to it) manifests itself in shape or appearance. But this apparition has no power whatsoever because the mentality or the mind of the individual – the ghost – is not there, is not present. In other words, it is a kind of a shell that is formed out of the ether under certain given conditions, quite often at certain times, and it has a limited power. It can only move in certain areas and under certain conditions and can only be seen, quite often, by people who are (without realising it) mediumistic or sensitive to the extent that they can see onto that vibration which is all around the Earth – which is very much used, often by spiritualist mediums, to link up and to tune in with spirits from other spheres. By this, I am trying to convey that a ghost is an entirely different thing to a spirit. You might say a 'ghost', which has no real substance and no real power, is a very strong thought vibration which has impregnated itself upon the atmosphere in a certain given place, invariably because at the time of the death of the individual, their thoughts were so strong and powerful that they left behind a memory condition which can be to some extent tangible, although the individual concerned has recently, or at some time when the happening of the passing took place, long since left.

With a lot of these hauntings, the poltergeist has no connection with the individual. It is a condition of the past which has registered itself very strongly upon the atmosphere, thereby being able to recreate in a given form, shape, and substance of a kind which has no actual physical power – material power – but merely an etheric condition, and cannot under any circumstances do any harm whatsoever to any living person; cannot in any way do anything or say anything or have any power upon any individual that may be conscious of its presence. You may find that in very old houses, castles and so on, that these apparitions do appear, and not necessarily are they alone. For instance, there are places where great battles have been fought, where sudden death has taken place en masse, and the thought-force has been so powerful, so much registered around and about that spot, that there are occasions when visually that battle can be seen again. In fact, the astral or the etheric world which intermingles with yours is in a sense a mirror. It registers and can show all manner of incidences appertaining to man's life, particularly the point of death. The Earth world is surrounded, completely and absolutely, by this etheric condition of life or substance, such as it is, which contains reflections of past events. In fact, one might say that every-thing that has happened of any consequence, individually and collectively to man, is still in the atmosphere.

Even the most ordinary of people may go to a house with the intent to buy that house or to live in that house in the future, and yet not necessarily be psychic, as is generally understood in the term 'mediumship', and on opening the door will sense and feel an atmosphere. Sometimes it is so strong that no matter how pleasant the house may seem and be in many respects, they would not buy it; neither would you have it as a gift, because in that house is a power of a kind which is so strong, so powerful, that no individual would feel happy. The walls are impregnated with the thought forces of individuals, or an individual, who has lived in that place.

It is perfectly true that we ourselves create our own atmosphere and that we are all individuals, and some much more powerful than others; and regarding our possessions when on Earth, our houses, our places of worship, and so on, you will find varying conditions. Usually, they are quite pleasant and liveable. But there are these places where deeds have taken place, things have happened to individuals which have so impregnated the very walls, and the atmosphere – even though the spirit has gone on in the spheres – has been left behind, which registers to such an extent that no-one feels disposed to live in those vibrations and conditions.

Unfortunately, the Spirit World knows so little about vibrations. Vibrations are always being quoted regarding séances. He says that he believes that science in our world today is gradually discovering much more about vibration: what it can achieve, what it can do, what it is. But even so there's a limit, I feel, to what science may discover about psychic forces; because psychic forces are, in themselves, unscientific from the material point of view. They are so powerful, too, and they cannot necessarily be harnessed in a material sense.

A house that retains powerful vibrations of thought forces is not easily altered or changed. Quite often it's a common thing when a house is reputed to be haunted to call in, perhaps, a local clergyman or canon or a dean or someone to exorcise. There is no such thing as being able to exorcise a power which manifests itself in etheric conditions unless the individual spirit is present. The only way it seems to me that a change can be brought about is not by exorcism but by the power of the individuals concerned, who may live in that building, to concentrate their thoughts in such a way that those thoughts will counteract the vibrations in and around the building; that they may release, as it were, those memory forces, those forces which in themselves have no substance but are purely mental conditions left behind by the entity that has gone ahead. In other words, by the power of thought you can change the vibrations of that building and clear it of its force, which may not necessarily be evil.

Regarding evil influences or evil spirits, it is very rare indeed that you have a place that is evil (if you accept evil in the sense that it is generally accepted). Individual forces from individual minds create certain conditions which are not always easy to change, easy to alter, but it can be done when you understand more about this subject of haunting. The etheric, the substance, and it is a substance, in which is registered all manner of things appertaining to the past, cannot necessarily be changed but it can be so affected by thought forces from your side, from your world, right thought forces of good, to counteract and disperse something which is unpleasant and unnecessary.

There is a vast difference between these so-called appari-

tions which have no real power than, for instance, to a haunting which is of an individual spirit. And where you have the individual spirit haunting a place or staying around a place or appearing at certain times in a place, that – because it has real substance behind it: the thought force and the power of that thought of the individual – is an entirely different matter altogether.

And it is possible to communicate with that spirit by mind and ask that spirit to leave and to help that spirit; because invariably they need help: they're Earth-bound and you can help them.

At 'Borley' the Rectory that was, and in the church itself, where there was a manifestation which was very real, was not of one person but of two. One was of a nun who for many years had clung to the place. She had been very ill- treated and had been seduced and her child had been destroyed in infancy and to keep her quiet she had been murdered; and, of a monk who was responsible. This happened many centuries ago and you would have thought that a soul would have, over many centuries, long since departed. This nun appeared at intervals, and she was anxious – one would have thought after so long a time that it would have been rather pointless – but nevertheless she was anxious for the skeleton, the body, to be discovered and of the child.

The monk himself committed suicide later that was hushed up. This is going back many centuries – somewhere round about nearly 400 years. Here there was no evil; there was nothing there which could be considered unpleasant. It was simply that from time to time she was drawn back to Earth by thought forces and memories of past events and of *the desire for justice to be done, and this strange idea, too, for the body to have been buried in hallowed ground, which was then considered very important. Since she herself was not buried in hallowed ground, it held her in some sense closer to Earth. She wanted to see this brought into being, this justice being done; but this is only one isolated case.*

There are thousands of authenticated cases of individuals who have seen manifestations sometimes of the individual concerned who is troubled in their mind and wants some matter put right that was left undone, or someone brought to justice for some deed that had been done against them, such as murder. Most of these cases are well authenticated, were individuals who were perturbed in their minds and could not find peace and rest and haunted certain places with a hope of either bringing justice into being regarding themselves, or to perhaps show where money had been hidden which preyed on their mind after death, or for some reason such as that.

But there is a vast difference between these individual hauntings by individual spirits than there is to these other apparitions that have no substance as such, which are merely etheric manifestations in the ether of thought forces long since, as far as the individual person's concerned, long since departed. Particularly in places like the Tower of London there are these etheric forces hovering around the building. It has also been well authenticated with individual soldiers, for instance, on duty who've seen apparitions without any shadow of a doubt – but they're not necessarily the individuals: they are thought force creations in the ether which at certain given times, under certain given conditions, can be seen, can be even spoken to. It is very rare that a ghost speaks. They have not the power of speech. But where you have an individual – that is an entity – who returns to Earth, they are sometimes able to register sound waves or to vibrate sound waves and make themselves heard, and they are audible.

Poltergeists are invariably individuals who are Earth-bound who do, by the power which they may have under the conditions which they exist in the place, are able to use various things to attract attention. Usually, you'll find there is someone in that household – quite often a young person -- who's full of vitality and power and psychic force, makes it possible for them to become more material in as much that they can either if they cannot be seen, they can use the power drawn from the individual in the household to move furniture or to throw things about. This is a deliberate attempt at communication; invariably not spiteful, very rarely spiteful, usually done in exasperation to attract attention to themselves, invariably because they wish something in that house to be discovered. It may be money that is hidden, or it could be, perhaps, even a body that has been buried, perhaps under the floorboards. There are many reasons and very good reasons why some spirits do return and haunt places, because they want something put right that is disturbing them. They cannot, as it were, rest or settle in their new environment; they are concerned with material things because those material things are very much on their mind. They realise that there's something that they want to put right and until it's put right, they do not feel they can leave the Earth world – they cannot leave without this matter being settled. I will give an example of a person that will die leaving money hidden perhaps in floorboards or something, and it worries them. They feel that they should have left a Will or indicated where this money was hidden and so on.

All manner of things causes people to be Earthbound and this is not necessarily a long-lasting thing. Usually, a person is not Earth-bound for a very long time because after a time, if they are not able to get in touch, eventually they begin to realise the futility of trying to do something in a material sense (which often they realise is impossible) to attract the attention sufficiently to make it possible for what it is they wish to convey to be understood, and they leave. But you do get the persistent types who will cling and will hold on and they will in consequence do everything in their power, particularly if they feel within themselves, it's essential that it should be attended to or done. Examples include the apparitions of horses, of dogs, of cats, even of birds: now these apparitions are not necessarily real from the point of view that the soul is present. Invariably these come under the category of etheric manifestations which are thought-force on the ether which at certain times is visible. These phantom horse-drawn carriages: they have no real substance. But there is a kind of reality in as much that they are seen and witnessed by people on your side, but they have no real substance. In fact, they are etheric reproductions of events that have taken place, perhaps hundreds of years ago which are very strong and powerful and continue to register, often for many years

There are some very amusing ghosts: ghosts with a great sense of humour. Sometimes, you do get individuals who have a wonderful sense of humour, and they do from this

*side endeavour to do things which cause perhaps some irrita-
tion or annoyance, but there is a sense of fun; because we on
this side, as you know, are not necessarily changed immediately by death. We are very much the same people – that's
one thing that I've discovered since I've been here, that this is
a world of reality.*

*Our world is a world of illusion in as much that so much
that goes on, that you accept as factual and real, to them is
very unreal apart from being factual. This is the world of
reality, and we have the attributes, and we have the defects
often that we may have had on Earth. (He made a joke
about those spirits don't suddenly become angels and that
they see the funny side sometimes of the goings on in our
world, particularly with individuals that we're fond of. At
certain times people come back from their side and they enter
your life, take an interest in what you're doing and, of
course, they can see more deeply than people on your side can
see, into the hearts and minds of others. And they do see
things which possibly the individual concerned endeavours to
hide very carefully from others, very successfully, but we see
the full person. They don't see just a façade and don't see
what people would like others to see and ignore the rest. They
see everything with a sense of fun. Sometimes individuals
from their side, who are by no means bad souls, do things to
try and jerk people in your world out of themselves, to make
them conscious of things which are more important, and to
make them think and act differently in their own personal
lives.*

*There is a reason and a purpose of hauntings on their
side. Sometimes it strikes them as rather funny when a cler-*

gyman starts to try and exorcise because no-one has the power to exorcise. I am quite sure the average clergyman hasn't a clue about this whole subject. In fact, clergymen do not have the vaguest notions about communication, about spirits. The average church man is very ignorant of the truths of life after death and has a vague belief which may be to him a reality, but there is no substance behind it to prove my statements. They come often to jerk out of themselves these very people who would exorcise us. Sometimes a haunting that may take place is deliberate in as much that it may bring in the clergyman and make him try to do something about it; but much more important to make him think more seriously about it – make him think more seriously about the possibilities of life after death and communication; to try and make him know there is something in the truth of survival.

A lot of things that go on which sometimes seem a little bewildering are done deliberately by our side. The apparitions that one sees occasionally as mentioned may be etheric remembrances of things past registered upon the atmosphere with no deep substance or reality of individual life. But a lot of the individual hauntings by spirits – apart from those who come because they wish to have something put right – a lot of it is done by souls from this side with the deliberate intention of arousing interest at certain times and at certain places to bring all manner of people to the realisation that there is something outside of your normal so-called existence. And if we can bring the church into it, who preach so much about life after death, and make them think more seriously about it, and the possibility of communication as well, then we're doing a jolly good job.

Spirit uses all manner of methods, all manner of ways, for trying to bring realisation and truth of survival to the world, and hauntings are quite often something which to us is a method and a way of arousing interest. And if we can get the local clergyman, or the canon or whoever he may be, into the house, or into the place, and get a lot of newspaper publicity about it, then we are setting people thinking and wondering, and also the parson himself (if it's possible to make him realise that he is also being used as a medium) making him think about survival and communication, we're on the right track of infiltrating truth in all directions. So, there are many reasons for this.

There are cases of individuals who are Earth-bound because of ignorance and because they're held so much down by material thoughts within themselves. They are materialists in life that they cannot fail to be – although in a sense apart from the Earth – materialists still, and they cling to those things they know and those conditions that they like, and for a time they live in a kind of illusionary world. They seem to have pleasure and fun and happiness of a kind out of making other people do the kind of things that they like doing. In other words, of course, they sometimes impinge themselves on individuals in your world and use them often for their own ends and that, of course, is bad and could in some instances be dangerous.

There are all manner and forms and conditions appertaining to hauntings, appertaining to apparitions and spirits. Spirit wants very much to give a much clearer picture of this because it is a very important thing for people on your side to know about.

Sitter: *Why do places go cold when a spirit's presence is felt?*

Harry Price: *I do not know. I guess in the process of drawing energy and power from, perhaps, individuals on our side make the manifestation possible that they may be taking something from the atmosphere which gives warmth. This is a feasible solution. There is always this and I have experienced it when on our side... of the coldness and the feeling as if there is something not normal or natural. But this may be due to a mental thing more than a physical – it may be a mental process which has a physical reaction, and the coldness is the reaction that you have. It may not be that the temperature changes; it may be an illusionary thing of change in temperature. Although it has been ascertained, I believe, by a so-called scientific method of noting that the atmosphere has dropped, and the temperature has dropped. As I have already said, there are these Earthbound souls who cling to individuals and use those individuals and often detrimentally.*

Sitter: *Do you know anything about the famous scientist, Sir William Crookes.*

Harry Price: *I don't know very much about this, but I have heard certain things said about him that weren't very complimentary. There will always be those who will, if they can by one means or other... some means or other... they'll use foul means to blacken the name of a person who has done so much to progress science and truth. It is the best thing to ignore these things because they will be accepted by the kind of mentalities that want to accept and discarded by those who are not of the same mentality. It's a problem. There is* *an old Chinese proverb: 'the tall trees gather the most wind'. I think that's perfectly true. The higher you become or the more famous you are, the more you become an 'Aunt Sally'. Do not worry too much about it because truth will out eventually. Regarding any criticism of a moral nature which I believe was suggested regarding Crookes, I think that one can ignore that; and that he would be party to something which was, well, fraudulent is ridiculous. He wouldn't risk and stake his reputation on something of that nature. A man who's got so much to lose – a good name – would not be party to anything, unless it was completely honest and straightforward. It is stupid that an intelligent person would refute and disagree with such a ghastly thing.*

THE AUTHOR'S EXPERIENCE OF POLTERGEISTS

I believe that I have experienced the power of a poltergeist where, during my marriage break-up, there were widespread plumbing issues through my matrimonial home. I believe that a poltergeist could have used the bad psychic energy between my ex-husband and myself to cause havoc, which I believe devalued our house. I have asked a world-class medium about this issue, and she agreed with me that it sounded like a poltergeist experience.

PART TWO
Pure Spirit

For my mother and father

Epigraph

'He that hearth you hearth me; and he that despises you despises me; and he that despises me despiseth him that sent me.

And the seventy returned again with you, saying, Lord, even the devils are subject unto us through thy name.

And he said unto them, I beheld Satan as lightening fall from heaven.

Behold, I give until you power to tread on serpents and scorpions, and over all the power of the enemy, and nothing shall by any means hurt you.'

— (LUKE 10:16-19, KING JAMES VERSION)

The Pure Spirit is inside of us. It is waiting patiently to be discovered. It is the pure joy, the unconditional *love, the energy that moves everything, the light of God. The Pure Spirit is inside all of us. It can be awakened. Also, it can be listened to, but not with our ears. Because it requires a spiritual stillness.*

— (SPIRITUAL EXPERIENCE, 2022)

CHAPTER 1
Spiritual Messages

I used to feel alone before I was aware of spirit[1] Now, I'm never alone as I've learnt how to understand and trust my spiritual guidance, which consists of my spirit guide Barnabas, who's a monk (a scribe), and my grandmother, Florence Marjorie Canning.

In this, my second part of this book, I hope to help you feel the love and power of spirit from reading the words within to help you realise you're never alone, there's always someone there for you – you just need to learn how to communicate with your spirit guides, which is easier than you think and certainly nothing to fear! It doesn't matter if you don't know who your spirit guides are; you just need to believe and trust in things that you can't see.

A person's life may consist of travelling many roads before they find their true pathway. Some people sadly never find their true pathway. I was close to remaining on the wrong path for the remainder of my life until my grandmother entered my life in the form of a dream 12 years ago. So, you see, dreams can come true!

My advice to you is not to be afraid and to try different pathways, as this is part of the fabric of life itself. Fortune favours the brave! I know for sure that if I hadn't been brave enough to fight for what I believed in, I wouldn't even have started my new spiritual journey, which has turned my dreams into reality!

In the first part of this book, *Spirit Writer*, I portray my spiritual journey and how I came to discover my spiritual gifts and understand my own spiritual journey so I can help others with theirs. Now I've come to terms with my past, my real journey has begun, and I'll now work towards fulfilling my destiny. This isn't about me any more, it's about my sharing my ability as a medium to help others discover their true destiny.

If you want to be able to hear spirit to enable you to receive guidance in your life, or if you just enjoy reading inspirational passages, then this part of my book is for you! My aim is to help you connect better with your inner self, your spirit guides and other people. Once connected, you'll be in a more positive frame of mind, which will enable you to work towards a better life for yourself.

If you've read the first part of this book, *Spirit Writer,* you'll be aware that I receive spiritual messages within my mind, and they flow out through my fingers and are typed on a keyboard, which is why spirit refers to me as a 'spirit writer'. (All such messages are shown in italics.)

Spirit is continually working to help people accept that there's an afterlife and no death, just a transition in form.

It also wants to help humanity with its understanding of life's trials and tribulations. Of those in your own life, some of them might have been intended to be part of your pathway and others might have been your own doing and shouldn't have happened, so you need to understand which is which. I didn't discover my own pathway until I was in my fifties, just because I listened to other people too much and didn't listen to my inner voice – my inner spirit. Remember, it's up to us whether we want to listen to our inner messages. We all have free will in the end!

Spirit has a language all of its own, and it isn't easy to put this language into words, as you need to understand not only the messages in your head (which are transmitted telepathically by spirit) but also the messages felt around your body. I'll try to put what I sense into words as best as I can within my messages in this book. All of us have a spiritual sensitivity, and by understanding this, you'll start to trust in your own inner messages, whereupon you'll find that you'll have a better understanding of your life path.

I'll try to help you visualise what it's like communicating with spirit, so you can recognise the same.

Imagine you're walking through a park and you hear the rustling of the trees and the babbling of a brook – this is how spirit communicates, like a child whispering in your ear.

On the earth, we listen to sounds that the world makes around us, and over our lifetime, we've learnt how to interpret those sounds. Our interpretation is based on whatever influences have surrounded us throughout our lives. The problem is that different people have learnt different information during their lives to interpret words in diverse ways to ours and each other's, and therein lies the problem. The background you've been raised within will have a bearing on your interpretation of different words and sounds, which in turn causes misunderstanding between mankind.

Spirit believes there will be a time when we'll all accept the same meaning of words, no matter what country you were born in and whatever life you've led; it believes everyone will interpret the words in the same way. One spirit message in this section of this book that relays this message eloquently is called 'Loneliness' (Chapter 9). It talks about how, at present, we have all developed our own interpretation of words, but there will come a time when we all will connect better with each other and be as one! Read this passage and you'll ll understand.

Spirit communication is so subtle. At first you think you're imagining it, but then, as time progresses, you realise that you are starting to know things that you shouldn't know. You then begin to realise that your knowledge must be coming from somewhere as you realise you have not learnt such knowledge during your lifetime. When you finally accept that you're getting guidance from somewhere, and then accept that this guidance is from spirit, it's truly a wonderful feeling. The word I'd use here to aid understanding is *'euphoric'*.

One crucial point to remember is that the finite (us) can't totally understand the infinite (spirit). We can only do our best to understand what spirit is trying to tell us. The subtleness of spirit's language is so gentle; that's why so many people struggle to hear it. You'll also become aware of a deep feeling of love within you, which is the love that spirit wants to share with you. However, you might not immediately understand what's being said to you, but this come with time and patience in a way that you'll understand. Dreams are one way that spirit may try to communicate with you, but there are many others. This was how they first communicated to me!

No matter how good or bad a person you think you are, spirit will help you understand what's right and wrong, and you'll be given a chance to right any wrongs in this life, without having to wait until the next life. Spirit wants everyone to realise they're in control of their own destiny, and it wants to hold you by the hand and guide you to a more fulfilling life, which will lead you closer to God.

Many writers throughout history are now coming forward, via mediums, to tell the world that they were spiritually inspired in their work, but they were scared to tell people in their lifetime. One such author is Sir Arthur Conan Doyle. Times are different now. We have freedom of speech, and we can all tell the world what we believe without fear of reprisal!

Spirit has now given me the strength to stand up for what I believe in. I did of course, realise I'd be taking a significant risk of being mocked and misunderstood in writing about my experiences, as the world as it stands is very science-based, but I knew that I had to take a chance, because if I didn't, it would make me unhappy!

At the beginning of my journey, I too was scared to tell people what I believed. Spirit came to me one night 12 years ago and gave me the confidence to stand up for what I believe and to live the life I was meant to live, not the life I'd lived for other people. Spirit also made it clear to me that it wanted me to understand my journey so I could help other people with theirs.

Every word I've written in this book is spirit-inspired and whispered to me from the spirit world – even the title of this book! It's clear to me that spirit is so anxious to spread its love, and I'm anxious to interpret this love in words that everyone around the world will understand, whether they're mediumistic or not!

Unbelievably, we're all mediums; it's just that we may not have learnt how to hear spirit yet as it's outside the normal five senses everyone has, which can be scary for anyone! Everyone will eventually realise the importance of words, the importance of the brotherhood of man, and that we're all created from the same spirit. As soon as everyone understands spirit's message, they'll start to understand each other, even when they speak in different tongues!

My spirit messages in this part of my book aren't in any order. They were relayed to me for a purpose, and it's for spirit to know why they're in the given order I'm merely a vessel who allows myself to be used as a channel!

I don't always know the purpose of the message or whom these messages were intended for, but this is normal for a medium or so I'm told by the experienced ones amongst us. Mediums are the key-holders who provide each of us with the key to our own door, but they can't guide each of us through our door, as we all need to go through our door on our own so we understand our own journey!

When I have an urge to relay spirit messages, I'm compelled to let spirit work through me, and I often rush to my keyboard to bash out what spirit is telling me. Some fellow spiritual friends tell me I should take more control of when I allow spirit to come through with messages, but I disagree. I feel thrilled and privileged to serve spirit and to serve God, and I consider it an honour for spirit to use me as a tool to help people interpret the word of God.

I aim to fill this part of my book with words of encouragement to help people understand the threads of life and not to fear transitioning from human form to spirit form. Even though I never know to whom my messages are directed, I believe and trust they'll mean many things to different people. Just because I've sometimes included my own interpretation of each message, the message might mean something else to other people. I suggest you use your instincts and life experience to consider your own interpretation!

Even if I only reach one person in the world with my spirit messages, I'll die a happy lady!

---

1. *In spiritualism, we use the word 'spirit' to mean the all-encompassing concept of this, as opposed to referring to individual spirits.*

CHAPTER 2

My memory of my father

Before my late father passed to spirit, I was told by spirit that it would be my duty to stand up before my family and talk about my father's life. Subsequently, spirit encouraged me to write the following words. This was one of the first occasions when I started to believe I was receiving messages. It was certainly my first experience of losing a loved one. Even my own mother, after hearing me at this funeral service, said I always know what to say! This was the nicest thing she ever said to me! I never told her that I was channelling spirit as she would not have believed me!

Although it was written for my father, I'm certain some of the words within will relate to many fathers around the world.

Isn't it the truth that you can live with someone for a lifetime, but it's only when they aren't with you any more that you realise their value?
That's the mark of someone who's special.
That's the mark of someone who deserves to be in the light and deserves to be with God.
To be remembered as someone who was always there to listen; to be remembered as someone who was always there to care; and to be remembered as someone who gave their time and dedication to others without ever asking for anything in return: this is how I remember my dad.
He was so special that no one realised his worth until they were aware he was no longer around.
I always remember that if he ever got a phone call from a member of his family who desperately needed his help, he never thought for a second about his own needs. He'd jump into his car and race to that person to give them aid, and he never wanted anything in return. That's how special my dad was, and he'll remain forever in our hearts and minds.
He was a devoted husband and father, and he told me on numerous occasions that he didn't want to leave his family, particularly towards the end of this life.
But dear Father, it's now your time to put aside your worldly shackles and rest forever more in the hands of God!!
Only your family knew of your suffering towards the end of your life, but despite this, you were always there when we needed you – sometimes pushing aside your own pain to aid others!
None of us got a chance to say goodbye; everything happened

so quickly. You drifted off to sleep and never regained consciousness.

Dear Father, you may have passed to the spirit world, but you'll be forever be in our hearts and minds, and so you will be forever with us – just as you wanted!

Rest in peace, Dad, until we meet each other on the other side...

CHAPTER 3

In memory of my mother

T hree years after the death of my dear departed father, I also lost my mother, and in the same way spirit made me aware to prepare for my father's death, it also prepared me for my mother's passing by helping me with the words to celebrate her life.

The first memory of my mother is how hard she worked to keep a lovely home for my sister and me. We never went without anything. In her words: she'd rather feed us and do without herself. People who knew her might have viewed her as a trifle pessimistic. The truth is that she was a realist and always tried to help people understand the situation they were in.
It's obvious that, from an early age, she'd learnt the meaning of 'family' and the importance of respecting money. Consequently, her memories stayed with her for a lifetime, and she endeavoured to pass those values on to her family.

In her later years towards the end of her life, much to her surprise, she was blessed with a grandson, Alexander, whom she adored, and it made me incredibly happy to see how much she loved him. In the past, she'd told me that she'd lost a boy herself, her first-born, and she wondered whether my son was in fact her first-born reincarnated. Spirit had told me that her first-born's name was Stephen. [Spirit gave me that specific spelling of his name.]

I always knew my mother was incredibly careful and never did anything in haste. Much to my surprise, I found a parking ticket on which she'd written my son's birth date and weight. She'd kept this in a drawer in her bedroom for 21 years, which I discovered shortly after her passing.

She always took hundreds of photographs of her one and only grandson; I'm going to put them together in an album, which I know would make her happy.

The people who knew my mother loved her. She had an air about her that would put at ease anyone who was in trouble. I don't doubt for a moment she'll be helping people in heaven now, and they're lucky to have her!

Despite the valiant efforts of Good Hope Hospital, which tried to revive her both at home and in the hospital, she died very suddenly, and they were unable to save her. The fact that her death was quick is the only consolidation her family can take from her sudden death.

I'm glad you're now at peace, Mom. We're all going to miss you!

Until we meet again...

* * *

Treasure special moments

T he aim of this passage is to help people treasure special moments. The story behind this passage is that I wrote it as a blog in 2015, but I never rediscovered it until 2022. Spirit wanted me to see how I'd grown, to provide me with encouragement to continue with my work, and to provide me with the passage I thought I'd lost.

At the time of writing *Spirit Writer* in 2022, I started to feel that spirit was guiding me again to continue with my second book (now Part 2 of this book). At this time, spirit reminded me of a passage that I'd written when I was at the beginning of my journey, whilst I was attending a Pilgrim's Progress Workshop at Erdington Christian Spiritualist Church.

During this class, the teacher told us to write a spirit-inspired message. I can remember placing this spirit message inside a folder, and I never thought about it again! I even forgot that I had put this online in a blog.

When I was thinking about this passage many years later, I told spirit in my mind that I'd lost it as I'd thrown my old folder away, and I never thought any more about it until one evening in 2022 when I was considering how to market my books.

Although I was used to be directed by spirit, to actually be directed to something online from many years ago even amazed me! I was directed to a blog which I had written many years ago. On reading the blog, I was shocked to find that it contained the message that I'd asked spirit to help me find. This is just one example of how spirit helps me with tasks I feel are impossible!

In this passage, spirit was telling me to treasure special moments. This message was relayed to me on the evening of our dear departed Queen Elizabeth II's funeral. This passage was lost between 2015 and 2022, and I was reminded of the same to remember this special *moment*.

A bird flies high up into the sky, soaring and swooping, surveying the world below. Through his eyes, we now look up high into the clouds.
On the ground below, small animals frolic in the fields. Water is babbling in the brook, for forever and a day. Children can be heard playing in the field, gurgling and squeaking. They try to catch butterflies, swooping their net. The moment is frozen in time, for they only know that moment. They can't see into the future, and they have little knowledge of the past. They'll remember that moment in time one day, when everything was so simple, so clear and so focused.

Their love and laughter can be heard for miles by the spirits above. They smile, and their hearts fill with joy when they see the children playing.
Freeze that moment in time forever and a day, so they may remember this moment for always...

CHAPTER 5

Spirit wants to speak to you

The aim of this passage is to help people who are mourning their loved ones and believe they'll never hear their voice again. Unknown to them, spirit is still around, and it will endeavour to help that person hear their loved one again!

I'm trying to speak to you. I'm trying to share my love. I'm trying to share my memories.
You think you can't hear me, but you can!
My words won't be words like you're used to. They'll be like the sounds of a rustling tree, so listen carefully as spirit messages enter and leave your mind quickly, so you must be alert.
You think I'm far away, but I'm closer than you think. I am but a thought away whenever you need my support.
You wish you'd said certain words to me before I passed.

Don't worry, I heard you speak those words to me in your thoughts.
I now feel what you felt, and I see what you've seen and what you see now.
I'm here when you need me and hear what you say to me.
I'll hold your hand when you need me and stroke your face to reassure you I'm around.
Always remember that you'll never be alone again!

CHAPTER 6

What spiritualism means to me?

T he aim of this passage is to describe how much spiritualism[1] means to me, which I hope will help people consider whether it is for them.

I used to follow the crowd.
I used to listen to what the world said to me. I used to believe what I was told to believe.
I used to cry when the world told me to cry and laugh when the world told me to laugh.
Minutes turned into hours, hours turned into days, days turned into nights, and nights turned into years, with my mind searching for answers to endless questions.
Years passed. I couldn't understand why there was so much I didn't understand and why I was constantly seeking new directions.
Then, one day, or I should say one night, spirit came into my life!

One night, one dream, one moment, and my life was changed forever!
From then on, I no longer listened to the person next to me. I no longer listened to the world. I listened to my inner self, my spirit, and no one can take that away from me – even if they don't believe me!
My inner soul. My inner spirit. I now feel the oneness with spirit, and I know I'll never feel alone again.
I've now accepted that I'm spirit, and that spirit has been with me my whole life, but I didn't take the time to listen! I'm happy that spirit is now in my life, which has helped me love myself again! I'm now no longer unhappy. I'm now no longer seeking answers, as the answers are whispered to me. I always had the answers, but I just didn't believe that I was worthy. I now know that I am! You too are worthy! Now that I accept that I'm one with spirit, and I take the time to listen, the love is always there waiting for me. I'm now complete. I am spirit....

---

1. Spiritualism is now recognised as a religion. Spiritualists believe that the spirit of a dead person can communicate with the living through a medium; for more details, see the website given in the reference (Spiritualists' National Union (n.d)

CHAPTER 7

The personal responsibility of words

T he aim of this passage is to remind people of the personal responsibility they have to help their children understand and respect the meaning and importance of words.

I'm sure that, at some point, we've all said the wrong words to someone we love or we've said the right words and seen a tremendous turnaround, not only in your life but in the lives of everyone to whom you're connected.

Think about all the words you've said and the words you've received during your lifetime, and consider the impact they've had on your life and other's lives. It takes only a second to say a wrong word and a lifetime to take it back!

I can remember a teacher told me when I was a child at school, 'You are never going to be...' This is the worst thing a child can hear at school, especially from an authority figure such as a teacher. This tells us that people in authority should be more mindful of their words than ever!

Some people don't realise the true power of words. They can start a war or stop a war.
They can express love or hate.
They can build bridges or destroy them.
They can be used to pray to your God or to blame God for your own misgivings.
They can write a story, or they can destroy a soul.
Music can be a beautiful sound. Music can be a horrid sound. The first will leave you with a feeling of euphoria. The second will leave you with a headache.
When handing out words, think about what they'll portray to those who receive them!
A baby's first words and every word thereafter that this child speaks will impact the world in ways you can't comprehend; therefore, you must teach them to appreciate the true power of words. Once your child has control over their words, they'll be able to conquer anything that may happen in their short lives. So, when teaching your child their first words, I'd suggest you think about how they might use these words in the future. This level of personal responsibility is huge, but it's so important for a child to understand the impact their words can have!
They can portray love or they can portray hate; which words would you like to receive? The first may make you smile. The second may leave you bitter.
They can make or break a court case: one wrong word could

cost you your freedom, with you then spending a lifetime in jail. This teaches us the importance of employing a good solicitor, who can use the right words to fight for your freedom!
I hope my words leave you with food for thought!

* * *

CHAPTER 8

The sea of life

T he aim of this passage is to compare the troubles and turmoil of life to the ebb and flow of the waves at sea, to help people understand the overall picture of one's life journey.

The journey of life is like a tiny boat on the ocean waves.
Some days, the water is like a mill pond, and you can glance at the water to see your own reflection.
At other times, the water is a bit choppy and cloudy, and you must use your oars to guide your tiny boat. Other times, the water can be as ferocious as a cat, lapping against the sides of your boat, and you wonder when the sea will ever be calm again.
Remember that challenging times may lie ahead, but these times will make you stronger – stronger to fight the unknown.

*Like the sea, the trials of your life might seem vast, but if
people stand together, it will feel like the trickle of a stream.
This standing together focuses on the 'brotherhood of man'
principle, which is the second principle of spiritualism.*

THE SEVEN PRINCIPLES

The Seven Principles[1] form the basis of the Spiritualists' National Union's spiritualism, and they help spiritualists to navigate and combine their spiritual and human
journeys. They provide a positive moral and ethical frame-
work upon which people can base their lives. They were
given to us through the mediumship of Emma Hardinge
Britten, and they are adopted by those who choose spiritualism as their religion. They are as follows

1. The fatherhood of God
2. The brotherhood of man
3. The communion of spirits and the ministry of
   angels.
4. The continuous existence of the human soul
5. Personal responsibility
6. Compensation and retribution hereafter for all
   the good and evil deeds done on earth
7. External progress is open to every human soul

* * *

1. Spiritualists' National Union (n.d) (See the website given in the Bibliography for more details).

CHAPTER 9

Loneliness

The aim of this passage is to help us understand that, at this moment in time, everyone gives different meanings to words, maybe because of their background or maybe because of the language they speak! Spirit is telling us here that it can see a time in the future when mankind will all speak the same language and we will all understand each other, no matter what background or country you come from.

When I spoke this message, it was taped by a German lady who told me she felt comfort from it as she'd been feeling lonely. You'll notice I said 'spoke' when I usually 'write' my messages. This lady taped my words as I spoke them.

Many people have many different thoughts.
Many people only listen to their own thoughts;
understanding them isn't always easy.

When there's understanding, there's happiness and no sadness. We should realise we're not alone.
Spirit sends love to us and words that are needed. When we're all aware, people will understand.
The knowledge comes down to everyone who's ready to receive it. Some people may question spirit intelligence, but the knowledge only comes to those that are ready for it.
Ask, and the true meaning of love will come to us, and then everyone will be together as one.
We'll be one voice, with no separation of language. We'll understand each other.
When people work together and stand together, they won't stand apart, and everyone will share the love.
Stop and listen. Stop and share!

CHAPTER 10

Reflection in the water

The aim of this passage is to help people to see what others see. Spirit is suggesting looking into a pool of water and glancing at your own refection. Spirit is telling us that, one day, we'll see what others see! Although this passage is short, it's very poignant!

Glance into the water; what do you see?
Glance into the water; what do other people see?
A time will come when you realise it will no longer matter
what you see; you'll only care what other people see. You'll
look into the water and see your brother, not yourself! When
that time comes, you'll finally realise that we're all the same.
You'll no longer wish to be better than your brother, because
we'll all have the same understanding of what's important.
That time can't come about until we start to care for one
another in the way in which we wish other people would care
for us. [This is the second principle, the brotherhood of man.]

*When this understanding comes about, there will no longer
be any fear. There will no longer be any hate. There will
only be LOVE!*
*You don't have to wait until you return to spirit before you
seek forgiveness and guidance; you can make changes now.
[This is the sixth principle: compensation and retribution
hereafter for all the good and evil deeds done on earth.]
Now is the time, and now is the moment...*

CHAPTER 11

Burn your candle brightly

The aim of this passage is to help people not to be scared and to stand up for what they believe, and to burn their candle brightly!

It was my grandmother who first compared me to a candle that attracts people to its light. She told me, during my spirit dream 12 years ago, that she couldn't look at me when I was a child because my light was so bright! She said that I must have thought that she didn't care for me, but this wasn't the case; it was just that my light was too bright for her to gaze upon for too long. I never forgot this message, and throughout my life, other mediums have relayed the same message to me, so I realised this message must be true.

The last time I heard someone refer to my light was at a Sunday service at my local church, when a well-known medium who sees auras (Jacqui Rogers) was instantly drawn to me. She told me that my light was filling the church and I must be a soldier of God. This took me by surprise, as before, only my grandmother had outright referred to 'my light'. Immediately, I knew that spirit was reminding me of my task upon the earth and my duty to God!

This is also a short passage, but I believe it's very meaningful...

Burn your candle brightly when you want others to see who you are!
Your light will attract people to you who want to bask in the blaze of your flame. When this happens, you'll no longer be worried about your own problems; you'll be more concerned about other people's problems, and this will help you forget about your own problems!

The more I think about this passage, the more I realise spirit is reminding me that the time has come for me to forget about my own problems and to start to guide others on their journey!

Accepting death as part of life

T he aim of this passage is to make people aware of what it's like to be on your deathbed and what kind of thoughts might be going through your mind as you lie quietly waiting for death to claim you. Some might consider this to be morbid, but spirit is trying to help us understand that we won't be alone at this time; we are just transitioning from the physical state to the spiritual state from whence we came. It's my belief that spirit is constantly reminding us that we need not fear death!

*You lie in your bed waiting for death to claim you. You lie in
your bed, scared of the unknown.
People visit you from your past. They come to tell you what
you mean to them. They come to tell you your true worth.
These are the spirits of your loved ones who are coming to
hold your hand on your final journey.
You're looking through a haze, and you're no longer certain*

what everything means. Trust what you hear. Trust what
you see.
Feel the love that's being brought to you.
Hold your loved ones' hands and let them guide you to the
light.
Don't be scared. Just let yourself drift into the sea of love and
light!

CHAPTER 13

Fear of the unknown

The aim of this passage is to help people not to be scared of the unknown.

Fear can be very destructive and hold us back from the journey that was meant for us. I now know this is what held me back for much of my life! On a positive note, if I hadn't felt fear, I wouldn't have felt the glory that was bestowed upon me later in life. Everything is for a purpose!

People want to believe there's more to this life, but many fear the unknown, so they're sometimes scared to look for it! There's only one way to stop fearing the unknown, and that's through knowledge – knowledge not just from people on the earthly plane who've had spiritual experiences, but also from learning to listen to your inner messages from your spirit guides, and from learning to trust your intuition.

A lack of knowledge breeds fear, which can be disruptive to your life and make you believe things that aren't true. You need to find out the truth to help you relieve yourself of this fear! I too feared the unknown at the beginning of my journey, and that's why I started to make a mental note of strange events in my life, so I could try to understand what was going on. I knew I was taking a chance that no one would believe me, but I had to take that chance, as spirit was trying to help me stand up for what I believed in so I could help others. I knew I was experiencing strange occurrences, and I became aware that I was remembering key events in my life, but I didn't know why at the time. As soon as I overcome my fear, with spirit guidance, I became strong!

It has taken me a lifetime to come to terms with the fact that I was experiencing spirit phenomena, so I decided to write everything down in the first part of this book *Spirit Writer* in the hope that it might help even one person who has experienced similar phenomena.

Spirit will try to help us in many ways; we just need to find the time to listen. I now know I took the wrong turns in life because I didn't make the time to listen. In the beginning, I saw what I thought were visions, which I now know to be spirit, but I'm hearing spirit more clearly now. Spirit knows that I'm now listening to it, and the more that I listen, the more it's using my abilities to write my many messages. Often, spirit will feature in our dreams, and if it believes you're listening to it, it will also try to communicate with you at other times!

I invite you to come to terms with what you're afraid of in your life and to take this fear by the horns!

* * *

CHAPTER 14

Memories and loss of the Queen

The aim of this passage is to help people realise the importance of memories!

My granddad (in spirit) has just reminded me of my own special memories of when he gave me my first homegrown tomato to taste and when he built me my first doll's house. These are a few of my special memories, so let's consider why some events become memories for us and why other moments are forgotten.

What defines a memory? What defines a special moment?
Why do we remember some things and not others?
Some might say we could be remembering things from a
previous life; this may be true. Our likes and dislikes appear
at an early age, so again, this may be why. We certainly like
things or dislike things for a reason. Or could it be the way
these occurrences are presented to us that determine whether
they become good or bad memories.

Whatever the reason, we remember our memories, it's certain they'll impact our future lives, be it for good or bad reasons. We might not understand those reasons at the time, but it's likely that we'll be reminded of them in our future to help us understand that things happen for a reason. Memories can also be a connection, or a bond, between loved ones – just like when my grandfather let me taste my first tomato. My grandfather is making me remember this bond at this time so he can remind me about the importance of memories and deep bonds that we should make with our fellow man.

I realise now that my grandfather is linking this memory theme to the memory of the loss of Queen Elizabeth II and reminding me to remember this moment, as it's a special moment and one I'll only experience once in my lifetime!

CHAPTER 15

What's in a name?

T he aim of this passage is to help people understand the importance of using a correct name tag to describe themselves to others so they don't lead others to believe something they're not.

Do you find that some people these days are giving themselves a name tag that often doesn't truly represent who or what they are? I'm inspired this evening to talk about being careful regarding listening to the wrong people when seeking spiritual guidance. You must listen to many people before you find the right person to help you understand your journey. I hope you gain something from this passage.

You must discover the right door to go through to change your life. Sometimes, you must go through quite a few doors before you find your ultimate door, which will lead you to your pathway, but don't let this dishearten you, because you'll eventually appreciate the end goal even more when you've experienced the journey!

Have you noticed how people are hung up on calling themselves a certain name, hoping that people will believe they have certain skills that are attached to this name. In the end, it doesn't matter what we call ourselves so long as our words and actions are said and done in good faith, and we don't deceive people into believing something that isn't true! People have the right to believe or not believe what you say, as we all have free will, so there's nothing wrong with this, but there are those who won't even consider what you say and poke fun without having true understanding!

You can give someone the key to their door, but you can't make them go through their door. If people don't believe what you say, aren't prepared to do research themselves to deepen their knowledge, and are being negative, then it's difficult to help that person find their way. Can you imagine how frustrating it must be for a spirit guide who's wanting to help someone, but they can't even begin to help until that person acknowledges them and isn't scared. That's how patient spirit is. Sometimes, spirit guides must wait a lifetime, but they'll never give in. They're persistent and they'll keep trying to help you understand in many ways. Remember spirit has no perception of time!

If you open your heart and mind to the spiritual side of life, you'll receive messages. These messages might come in the form of dreams or they might be in the form of sending someone to help us understand a situation. I know this to be true, as that's what happened to me on my journey: spirit sent many people my way to help me believe in the existence of spirit and to believe in my spiritual gifts so I could help people who were drawn to my light.

At this moment in time, many people are claiming they have spiritual abilities, and they call themselves many names, and each person who visits them is expecting a different thing from their visit. However, what they expect often comes from their perception of what has been said and experienced throughout their life – the contents of which might be right and might be wrong. This is the reason people are dissatisfied with spiritual guidance given by people who claim they are this or that. They're trying to understand situations without having enough knowledge to make their own decisions!

I believe spiritual guidance should be focused on spiritual philosophy, for only when you understand this will you understand and eventually believe in your pathway. The essence of spiritualism is 'philosophy' and only by understanding this will you understand the words of God. Remember, finding your pathway starts with trying to find your key, and once you've found your key, you must then find your door to use that key in. Don't forget, it's you who must go through that door on your own, which can often be a long path!

Following a spiritual path is not easy, but I'm sure of one thing: once you've found your door, you'll find happiness and love that you've never experienced before!

Don't fear trying a few door handles until you find the door that's meant for you!

* * *

CHAPTER 16

The joy of music

T he aim of this passage is to help people
appreciate the joy of music.

Throughout the whole of my life, I've loved
music; I've used it as an escape from the world around me
and escape from things I didn't understand. I now know
that the sounds I was trying to block out at an early age
were the sounds of my spirit guides, who didn't wish me
harm; they came to show me the way!

Due to my lifelong love of music, I feel it only fitting
that I pay homage to the many people of our time who
either sing or play an instrument, and in doing so, they
bring so much joy to others, helping people to forget their
troubles and join with their brothers and sisters in a
moment of peace and serenity!

*Oh how sweet the sound of a melody to herald a moment in
time!*
Forget about your troubles and let your mind dance to the

sounds of the angels. Let your foot tap to the rhythm and let your body sway from side to side.

Don't worry if you can't dance. Don't worry if you can't sing. No one will be watching you, except your God. No one will be listening to you singing, except your God.

Sing and dance like your life depends on it. Bob and weave. Tip and tap your feet. Float around the dancefloor and let your heart sing with joy.

Forget who you are for a moment. Pretend you're a king. Pretend you're a princess.

Swing and sway, moving your partner this way and that. You're whoever you want to be when you let your favourite music float around your mind like the sea ebbs and flows on the seashore.

Bow your head in reverence to the masters of the world of music because they deserve respect for connecting people in many special ways, helping people forget their physical self for a moment and reminding them that they are spirit without them even realising it!

CHAPTER 17

Time

The aim of this passage is to help people appreciate and value time.

When do we get an awareness of time? This is a good starting point because it's only when we get that awareness of it that we become anxious about the passage of time and are concerned we won't have enough time to do this or that. For sure, the older we get, the more anxious we become about time running out; we start to regret what we haven't done with our lives, believing we'll never get a second chance to put things right!

It certainly isn't possible to go back in time, but it is possible to embrace the here and now, and you don't have to wait until the afterlife before you decide that you want to put right wrongs of the past and change your life for the good! In fact, by taking control of your life now, you're making an early start on transforming your life when you return to your spiritual existence. *[This is the sixth princi-*

ple: compensation and retribution hereafter for all the good and evil deeds done on earth] No matter whether we're good or bad, we all return to spirit in the end, because that's where we came from and that's where we'll return to – remember we're our own judge and jury!

When I was at a crossroads in my life 12 years ago, I wanted to know the reason why I was so dissatisfied with my life, despite having fulfilled all the usual earthly desires people have. My life started to change when I started asking questions to which I subsequently received answers.

I thought I wasn't aware of spirit from an early age, I now realise that spirit has always been with me, trying to help me find my way. Of course, at the time, I didn't realise that my many questions were being answered. It was just that I wasn't listening and believing!Now, at the tender age of 57, I realise that it's only when I ask questions that I receive answers!

Remember when I spoke about my concern about losing a lovely spirit message that I wrote in 2015, which I believed I'd never find again? It was only when I had this question in my mind regarding where this passage was that it appeared on my screen shortly thereafter. Even though I'm now becoming more aware of how spirit is working with me, it wasn't until this moment that I realised my questions were really, truly being answered – all I needed to do was trust!

I've seen and felt many wondrous things in my lifetime, but I'm still learning to understand how spirit is working with me. The fact that I'm now writing about time indicates to me that spirit doesn't want us to be frightened of time, but that we are to embrace it to remind us to focus on what we want to achieve in the time we have left on the earthly plane, and thereafter when we return to spirit!

Part of our earthly existence is about learning; we never stop learning, and making mistakes is part of learning. So if you find you've hit a crossroads, take a breath, take time to decide which direction to go in next, and follow the direction you believe is right for you. You'll find that, by taking stock and asking for guidance, it will give you time to consider your way forwards or your next step.

Imagine for a moment that you're walking through a beautiful, wooded area with a trickling stream beneath your feet.
Behind you are the stepping stones of the past, and in front of you are the stepping stones of the future.
If you've come to a crossroads and wonder whether you should go this way or that, stand for a moment on the stone that's your turning point and look ahead at the obstacles in front of you.
But don't forget how far you've come, as it's because of your past that you are where you are now, be it right or wrong.
Only you will know whether your past was right or wrong. It is for you to consider before you move on.
You have personal responsibility for your life, and you should not blame others for your mistakes.

. . .

In my case, I didn't fully appreciate my journey until I came to a pathway later in life, and I realised the reason that I was being inspired to remember my life was so I could understand my future!

CHAPTER 18

The wonder of life

T he aim of this passage is to help people fully appreciate the wonder of life and all it entails!

I stand on the precipice of life, looking down upon the world and gazing high into the sky in one fleeting glance. At this moment in time, I can feel no pain, no sorrow. I stand in awe, admiring how boundless and wondrous the world is.
Every crevice of land is teaming with life.
Every drop of sea is teaming with life.
Every breath of air is teaming with life.
Nothing is wasted in nature. Life and death are so intertwined that, sometimes, it's difficult to know when life starts and when it ends; but does the animal kingdom worry? No.
The swoop of the wand of Father God might seem ruthless to mankind, but mankind must remember there's a time to

live and a time to die; that's the circle of life. Animals don't worry where the next meal is coming from; they see their babies surrounding them, and they know instantly they must go out into the world and gather food to fill their bellies. The chicks grow into strong birds, and their mother dies, but the chicks don't worry about the death of their mother; they lift their tiny wings and fly high into the sky just like their mother taught them, and they start the circle of life again.

We can learn a lot from Mother Nature!

CHAPTER 19

Be like a rose

T he aim of this passage is to help people realise how important they are to God!

I'm being shown a rose – a beautiful, red rose – and I'm reminded how easy it is to exist as such. It's this simplicity that spirit wants us to think of when we're troubled!

Being a rose is so simple and so beautiful.
Whatever the rose wants, Mother Earth provides. It doesn't
have to think about what to do, and what not to do. It
doesn't have to ask for what it needs.
If it needs rainwater to drink, it's provided by Mother
Earth.
If it needs nourishment, it's provided by Mother Earth.
If it needs sunlight, it's provided by Mother Earth.
If it wants to pollinate other roses, it doesn't consider how or
why; Mother Earth sends a bee to dart from one rose to

another, spreading the beauty of nature throughout the world!

If the rose wants to show its beauty, it simply opens its petals and shows its beauty with pure innocence. It never asks for anything; it doesn't need to as everything is provided by Mother Earth for the rose to sustain its beauty.

Wouldn't it be nice if we could live our lives as simply as the rose?

Wouldn't it be nice if we had no worries, and everything was taken care of by Mother Earth? It is. It's just that we don't appreciate the beauty of what gifts we have until it's too late. If everything is provided for the rose without it even asking, why do we doubt that everything will be provided to us, as in our form, we're closer to God than the rose is? The rose doesn't doubt or question, and yet it flourishes for a moment in time, but what beauty it displays in the little time that remains!

It simply exists.

It simply is.

We come from the Earth and we return to the Earth, just like the rose, and yet we have so many questions and so many doubts despite being provided with gifts that the rose will never have – yet a rose doesn't doubt or cry!

Wouldn't it be fine if we could believe without wanting proof?

Wouldn't it be fine if we could accept the help that's available to us without doubting?

Walk through a rose garden, touch the petals and smell the sweet perfume surrounding you, taking care not to touch the thorns!

[Here spirit is telling us to live our lives: with an air of simplicity like the rose, but to always be aware that we're personally responsible for our actions, which is what spirit means by 'take care not to touch the thorns'.]
Nature surrounds us with beauty every day, yet we don't always appreciate it. Take the time to appreciate the beauty of nature and don't question, just accept – like the rose!

CHAPTER 20

The place of God

T he aim of this passage is to help people understand the place of God in the religion of spiritualism. (This is the first principle of spiritualism).

Everything in nature has a place, a start and an end.
A time to be born and a time to die.
God and the Natural Law play a key role in spiritualism.
From considering the accounts of many mediums of the past,
my own experiences and my connection with God, I believe
that he doesn't want to be seen as the vengeful God of old, as
portrayed by the Church. He wants to empower people to take
responsibility for their own actions and to take charge of
their own destiny, embracing their fellow men as 'equals' no
matter what their position.
It's also clear that it's only by being 'of one mind with our

*brothers' that the world will understand the meaning of
God and the Natural Laws of the Universe!*

Even before I was aware of my spiritual connection, I
always felt an inner connection with God, despite being
brought up in a family who didn't believe in the same. I
never realised at that time that the knowledge being
bestowed on me, even from an early age, was from God
and my spirit guides.

I used to think that I had a vivid imagination as a child,
as I had no one around me with spiritual knowledge to
compare my knowledge with!. It took me most of my life
to discover the truth – the truth about love, the truth
about life and the truth about family – not just our own
family, but the family of our *'brotherhood of man',* whom
spirit tells us we should try to connect with to enable us to
become closer to our *Father God.*

*There's no need to fear God.
There's no need to fear birth.
There's no need to fear death.
There's no need to fear anything – that's spirit's message. At
all times, we're with our loved ones, who are surrounding us
with their love and guidance should we ever need it; and
when it becomes time for our transition to return to our
spiritual existence, they'll be there waiting for us in the light,
holding out their arms to take us on the next stage of our
spiritual journey!*

* * *

CHAPTER 21

The world of dreams

The aim of this passage is to portray how important the world of dreams has been in helping me understand spirit messages.

As a child, I couldn't wait until bedtime when I could drift in the land of make-believe. Many a time I didn't know what was real and what was a dream state.

To this day, I'm still an avid dreamer, and since I've learnt that spirit comes to us in our dreams, I appreciate this special time even more! As dreams are so important, both to me and spirit, I felt it important to write a few words on the world of dreams!

The world of dreams is a world of make-believe.
It's a time in which your mind can drift and your body can rest.
It's a time when you can forget who you are and imagine who you'd like to be.

It's a time when you can become closer to your loved ones.
It's a time when you become closer to your God.
In your dreams, you lose your inhibitions and you let go, like
a puff of smoke. Your spiritual body is no longer held back by
your physical body, so it can be spirit once more.
Without even realising it, our bodies constantly yearn to
return to spirit; spirit describes returning to the spirit world
as being just like when you take off your coat.
We aren't scared of taking off our attire, and so we mustn't
fear being released from our physical body and returning to
our spiritual body!
Spirit tells us the importance of learning and to let go of the
past so we can be free to live our future.
Let go of the past.
Let go of our physical self.
Only when we learn how to do this will we hold hands with
our loved ones again and, eventually, hold the hands of
our God!

* * *

CHAPTER 22

The importance of healing

Spirit has shown me here how beautiful healing is, and that we must hold it gently within our hands and gaze at it like it's an iridescent pearl.

The aim of this passage is to help people understand the importance of *'healing'* in the world.

During my mediumistic training, I've had moments when I believed I was struggling to hear spirit clearly. I couldn't understand how I was struggling to give messages in class, often just standing silently, my fellow classmates wondering why, and when I returned home to my sanctuary, my home, I'd have conversations with spirit!

I always remembered that several mediums had told me the importance of letting go of the past to move forwards, and only now do I realise I was being given good advice. After this guidance, I felt the urge once more to be available to talk to spirit – not just to listen, but to talk!

I now realise how important *'healing'* is for me – not just to help others, which I've always wanted to do, but to heal myself! By healing myself – by which I mean releasing the past from my mind.

At the time of writing the first part of this book, Spirit Writer, I believed that writing about my past was an important part of my healing process, but I now realise that it is an even greater part of my healing journey, as through it, I am helping people understand the part that God plays in everyone's life!

Since my healing practicals, which have been part of my healing course, I've noticed my connection to spirit has increased tremendously.

I've been aware of spirit for a long time, but I've sometimes had problems hearing everything spirit told me. I was always aware of spirit's presence, but I sometimes found it difficult to hear its messages and I now realise the reason why was that I needed to heal and I needed to learn to listen with greater intensity to spirit!

I recognise now that the way spirit likes to work with me is like a mother would hold a baby – this is the only way I can describe it!

Over the last 12 years, many mediums have told me healing was important to me, but I've had to find out for myself just how important!

In the beginning, I didn't know whether healing was for me, but since completing my healing training I recognise that it is part of me – part of my spiritual make-up.

Once again, spirit has shown me the way to use my spirit writing to help me listen to its words. I can't believe how clearly I can now hear spirit. Sometimes, I have a tear running down my face as I feel the beauty and the divinity of spirit when it relays messages to me!

CHAPTER 23

Previous lives

The aim of this passage is to help people understand that we all have a purpose in life, and it's part of our journey to understand that purpose!

When you think of your present life and what you consider has gone right and what has gone wrong, don't be too harsh on your- self. When we make the transition from spirit to physical, we're given choices to achieve certain goals!

For years, I had a heavy heart because I was thinking I'd made a mess of my life, and that's why, 12 years ago, I said many a prayer asking for guidance on how best to conduct the rest of my life. It's only now, midway into my healing teachings, and after my dear grandma whispered in my ear again, do I realise that everything I've gone through and the distance I've travelled, whether painful or joyful, was planned for me before I even came back to exist as 'Wendy'.

Spirit wanted me to understand life in order that I could help other people on their journey, and it was only when I had a lifetime's worth of experiences that I realised everything was meant to be!

I'm not saying there won't be occasions when you might go down the wrong road due to earthly influences, but I think it's safe to say that – no matter how painful this might be to hear, so please forgive me – most of your journey was more than likely planned, and it was your ultimate goal to understand something you didn't understand from a previous life.

So dear heart, don't feel too bitter of heart when wondering whether the mistakes in your life were all due to yourself. Be joyful, as I genuinely believe that, if you're reading my words, it's because you were meant to be reading my words. Please don't think I'm being overzealous with this remark.

I was meant to write. I am a spirit writer.

I was meant to teach.

I was meant to hold your hand to help you realise you've come a long way if you're reading my words!

If you realise where you've gone wrong, you should have a good idea which road to go down next. Forgive me if my words sound hard to grasp. Feel my words within your heart and remember that you can only go forwards – you can't go back. Move forwards with love and don't look back. Believe in your heart that you're now on the right road!

* * *

CHAPTER 24

Do animals have souls?

The aim of this passage is to help mankind understand the place that animals have within the world!

Why do we foolishly think we're the only presence on the earth that has a soul? We boast about our intelligence and then demonstrate our lack of compassion for others, which suggests there's something missing in our spiritual make-up! I liken the beauty and simplicity of animals to a newborn human baby who doesn't understand what they're feeling, what they're seeing, what they're hearing, and their need for food and drink. Despite all this lack of knowledge, they instinctively demonstrate they know what's right and wrong, and they hold their little arms open with unconditional love for their parents, just like our loved ones open their arms for us, welcoming us back into the light!
Spirit suggests we'll need to return to this inner knowing if

181

we're to truly prepare for our return to our spiritual existence, so as to show to the great divine that we've learnt compassion for our fellow man during our earthly existence. Consider how dogs can be trained to sniff out substances, to catch criminals, to provide company to old people, or to serve people with disabilities (such as those who are blind), helping them discover a new life and keep them free from harm. I'd challenge anyone who doubts that these animals have love in their hearts and that they don't each have a soul.

They might not be able to talk, but they demonstrate daily that they want to please their owner and they're willing to serve and devote their life to their owner.

They show their unconditional love in ways that many humans couldn't possibly comprehend, never asking for anything in return, and making us warm and fuzzy inside. Whatever happens in the earthly world, animals seek to show us the way without asking for anything in return!

CHAPTER 25

Through the eyes of a wolf

The aim of this passage is for mankind to consider what it's like to be a wolf. This passage demonstrates once more the unconditional love that spirit has for us and suggests picturing yourself as a wolf cub to understand what's important to them!

It's another example from nature of the 'brotherhood of man' principle [the second principle].

My first memory: huddled close to my mother's teat, her soft skin and fur enveloping me.
I chomp away, filling my mouth full of her life-preserving milk, the excess dribbling around my gaping jaws, with my eyes tightly shut as I savour the taste.
I gulp for air in between, filling my mouth with sweet nectar, the nectar of the gods.
My siblings surround me, fighting for the best position.
I notice that I feel stronger and stronger as the moon above

rises and falls.
I notice that sounds around me are becoming more distinct
and new smells are filling my nostrils, sending visions into
my mind that I'm beginning to understand.
Dominance prevails amongst my kind, the weaker following
the stronger, but that doesn't mean we don't care for one
another.
As we become stronger, we play-fight amongst ourselves,
demonstrating to each other who'll be the next leader.
In our world, we must prove we're worthy to be the leader,
but our dominance has a purpose and is not cruel like it is in
the world of men!
As our legs grow long, as our ears prick up, as our snouts grow
and as our fangs get more pronounced, our appetite grows for
more sustaining meat to fill our bellies, making sure no one
goes hungry.
To the outside world, we must appear to be ferocious,
scrabbling for our next meal, but only we know how gentle
we are, guiding and nurturing our fellow pack members, the
stronger protecting the weaker. (This is the closeness that
spirit wishes us to have with our fellow man and refers to the
second principle: the brotherhood of man.)
We soon learn the importance of the moon, and how we stay
connected with our pack by sending mesmerising howls into
the night sky.
Our howls not only help each member of the pack to be aware
of each other's location, but also serve to remind each other
that we're all as one!
To us, that sound is important because it makes us feel
stronger when we're together as one!

CHAPTER 26

The tree of life

The aim of this passage is to help people understand the circle of life.

When a seed was placed in my mind a number of years ago about the Tree of Life, its connections with Christianity and its even deeper roots with the Kabbalah, I became increasingly fascinated with what the *Tree of Life* represents. I knew it was portraying something special, but it would take me many years before I fully understood what it signifies. For this reason, I'll connect with spirit here to help us get a deeper understanding of it.

The Tree of Life represents all aspects of life and has been
referred to from the beginning of time.
Its branches. Its roots. Its fruit.
It's both good and evil at the same time. Just as man is good
and evil at the same time.
It reaches high with its branches, and it touches God.

*It reaches low with its roots, seeking out man-made desires.
It bears fruit in the summer sun, which represents
mankind's need to reach high up into the sky for the fruit of
the Lord.
The tree can only bear fruit if it reaches up high, so we too
can only taste the fruit if we reach high into the sky, aiming
for the sun, the stars and the moon.
The bark surrounding the tree grows thicker and stronger, so
we must do the same.
Our path will never be an easy one, but how sweet the fruit
will be if we nurture our seed – the seed that was planted by
our Lord – and it's for us to nurture that seed so we too can
become trees. (This relates to the personal responsibility
principle.)
In the midnight sky, the moon and the stars dance, filling
the dark void.
The light will always prevail and swallow up the darkness,
but a tree needs to be nurtured for it to blossom, and it can
only be nurtured by the light of the Lord, without which it
will wither and die.
So, we too will wither and die if we don't stand firm and
strong, waving our arms in the air like a tree waves its
branches in the cool breeze.*

CHAPTER 27

The connection between the two worlds

T he aim of this passage is to help people understand the connection between the spirit world and the physical world.

Spirit inspired me with this title, showing me two planets displayed on my computer screen so I'd understand the close connection between the spirit world and the physical world.

Spirit communication is very visual for me, and it often shows me images that it knows I'll understand. It works with me this way, as it knows I have a pictorial brain. It will work with you on whatever level is appropriate, so you'll understand what it's saying to you.

Spirit sees no barrier between language and culture; it will communicate to you in a way that you understand. Spirit wants all humanity to develop the same understanding so we recognise that we're all one, and if we hurt our fellow humans, we're hurting ourselves.

Spirit is inspiring me to write about how close the

spirit world is to the physical world, without you even realising this. People fear what they think is the unknown. However, what they think is unknown is, in fact, known because it's part of you without you even realising it!

My grandmother reassured me a long time ago that I'd start to become connected to the spirit world. When she told me this, it was only natural that I was initially scared, but she instantly sent love to my heart and mind to demonstrate to me that she'd give her life for mine if she had to. I have no doubt at all now that the love between my grandmother and me is boundless and will be so until the end of time. She has never shown herself to me in spirit form because, in her words, 'I never scared my children when I was alive, and I won't scare them now!'

Those in the physical world are now reaching high and low for answers to understand what's going on around them, so they've got more control over their lives, but they should be looking inside themselves as well. We're all made up of both a physical and a spiritual presence, and as the physical presence withers like an autumn leaf, your spiritual presence will remain infinite.

I know that spirit won't falter in helping mankind understand how beautiful each person's spirit presence is, and that we should nurture this as a farmer nurtures his crop, season after season!

Spirit surrounds the physical world, and the sensitive among us will sense this when they are ready, and not before. It has been like this since the beginning of time, and it will remain like this until the end of our days...

CHAPTER 28

Barnabas – my life and my guide

The aim of this passage is demonstrate the role that my spirit guide, Barnabas, plays in my life.

Many years passed before I knew who my main spirit guide was. He first made me aware that he had religious significance and left it at that. I never pushed him any more as I knew he'd tell me when the time was right.

Even before he made me aware of his presence, since I was a young girl I'd always felt I had a deep religious yearning inside me. This concerned my family, and I'd frequently hear them talking about how concerned they were about my obsession with God. The question in their minds was that they weren't religious, so why was I?

As time passed, I accepted what my guide told me. I knew one day he'd tell me his name and his significance in my life when he believed the time was right.

I first became aware of him when I was attending a spiritual awareness class at Erdington Christian Spiritualist Church, 12 years ago. One week, we were asked to think about our spirit guides and three guides appeared to me, with the major one calling himself a monk. I also knew that the second one also had a religious significance, and I was aware she was a nun. The third was an Indian medicine man, who was also deeply spiritual. No wonder I felt religious when I had all these guiding me!

As the years passed, the monk told me his name was Barnabas, but it wasn't until I started mediumistic training years later at Sutton Spiritualist Church that he started to make me more aware of his presence. During this time, a couple of Arthur Findlay College mediums also told me of his existence and of his religious and healing connection. I was told that he admired my positive attitude to life despite my troubled life!

When I finally accepted my role was to be a healer, I started to become more aware of how much he wanted to use my healing ability. He never failed to make me aware of his name, telling me constantly he was *'Barnabas'*. Eventually, I decided I needed to know more about him, and he told me that he was an early Christ- ian, one of the prominent disciples of Jerusalem.

Oh Barnabas, thank you for connecting with me!
Thank you for helping me understand my healing gift!
We're stronger together as one...

Barnabas has now made me aware it's time to draw *Pure Spirit* to a close. Now I'm more aware of his presence, I feel stronger for it, and the beauty of his healing energy flows through me like a cool summer breeze!

I'm also being made aware of the Bible quotation I've placed at the beginning of this part to help readers understand that God will stand by you if you stand by him...

The second passage focuses on the title of this section, Pure Spirit, and explains that pure spirit is inside each of us, it just needs to be awakened!

PART THREE
Spirit Healer

To all my healing guides who work with me everyday. May they continue to guide me and enable me to connect to their healing energies...

Epigraph

Healing takes courage, and we all have courage, even if we have to dig a little to find it.

— *TORI AMOS*

Although the world is full of suffering, it is also full of overcoming it.

— HELEN KELLER

Love is the most important healing power there is.

— LOUISE HAY

CHAPTER 1

The beauty of healing

I n this my third part of this book, I am now going to tackle the importance of healing, not just the healing as we know it today, but healing methods that have been forgotten about from the past, some of which are the roots to modern day medicine!

Healing is now an important part of my life, as I am now a working healing medium, and as such, I believe that healing should be an important part of everyone's lives. We all have a personal responsibility to keep healthy, both physically and spiritually!

Let's hope, as time moves forward, man will continue to understand the connection between his physical and spiritual existence, and that *healing* by whatever means, will be the norm!

MIRACLES DO HAPPEN!

We live in a world that wants answers to problems immediately.

We live in a world where they're no shortage of people trying to make money from quenching this desire.

We live in a world where people believe others easily, without examining the facts.

We live in a world where films, the word of the press and social media take precedence.

What do all these words mean? They mean that not everything that happens in life can be proven, and that miracles *CAN* and DO happen, every single day!

Healing is one such miracle, no matter whether it is performed by the medical profession, or by alternative methods.

One thing that is certain, all methods of healing have *roots*, and it is these *roots* that I will be examining in this section.

Without pioneers of the past, our present and our future might be very different!

ROOTS OF MODERN DAY MEDICINE

Traditional medicine has evolved from discoveries of pioneers of the past. If it wasn't for them, we wouldn't have the knowledge and technology that we have today.

Doctors insist that their knowledge is *scientific*, but some enlightened folk would question where the knowledge of these pioneers came from! There are many theories to this!

Did the knowledge come from God?
Did the knowledge come from outer space?
To understand the past, is to understand the future...

These may seem like humorous questions to some people, but to others, who believe in such things, they are a reality! I don't think we will discover the answers to these questions for a long time, but we can at least *contemplate* these mysteries!

Ancient civilisations like the Egyptians appear to have had knowledge beyond their years, but for some reason this knowledge was lost over time!

Does it really matter for us to be aware of where this knowledge came from? I think it does, as until we understand and appreciate what has made humanity as it is today, we surely cannot progress!

Surely, man cannot be so naive to believe that our pioneers did not have inspiration from a higher source!

MODERN DAY MEDICINE

The medical profession, as we know it today, are able to cure ills which shortened the lives of many of our ancestors. What is the norm today would have been miraculous decades ago! Now that we can live longer, due to the wonders of medicine, it is certain that more problems will come our way. It is these problems that we will have to solve one by one in the future by using every method of healing that we have at our disposal!

ALTERNATIVE AND COMPLEMENTARY METHODS OF HEALING

Modern day medicine now accepts that, in certain circumstances, complementary methods of healing are needed where traditional medicine has not been successful. What, or should I say who, influenced the medical profession to make this decision?

As a medium, I am completely aware that spirit has influenced my life. So, if it has influenced my life, it is a possibility that it has influenced the lives of important men in the medical profession!

Harry Edwards (healing extraordinaire) believed strongly of the existence of *divine intelligence* from the spirit world, and his beliefs are very persuasive. If he is correct in his theory, it suggests that man *IS* being guided, and that some men sense this guidance more than others!

If you have read the first section of this book, *Spirit Writer,* you will be aware that I started to become spiritually aware after a *dream.*

I am no historian, but I do know that men throughout history (through mediumship) now claim that they were also influenced by dreams!

Little did I know at the time that my dream would change my life, and the lives of everyone that is connected to me beyond all recognition!

. . .

HEALING AND THE WORLD TODAY

The world today is buzzing with the word *'healing'*, but does everyone understand the different forms of healing which are available?

Healing is now part of everyday life, whether people believe in it or not. People can no longer claim that healing does not exist, as many testimonials are available around the world, some of which are described in Harry Edwards' books. Testimonials within his books prove that miracles do happen!

Some of the people he healed were without faith and so turned to alternative methods of healing to seek a cure for themselves and their loved ones when the medical profession were unable to provide a cure!

PIONEERS OF THE PAST

There have been many pioneers of the past which have led to the acceptance of alternative methods of healing, one of which is Harry Edwards. I will consider how these pioneers drifted into healing, what they accomplished in their lifetime, and what impact they have made on *the World of Healing.*

UNUSUAL HEALING METHODS

As well as the well-known methods of healing, there are many more unusual methods such as by sound and colour, which I will consider, amongst others, to enable you to make a better informed choice as to which is suitable for you!

I would not, however, be doing my duty as a healer if I did not stress the importance of always going down the traditional medical path first before considering alternative and complementary methods.

WHAT MAKES A HEALER?

Believe it or not, we ARE all healers, but only certain people are able to use healing techniques. Why is this so? To this end, I will consider tell-tale signs that you might be a healer in Chapter 13.

Never think that there are too many healers, and that the world does not need another! If you have the gift of healing, it *is* for a purpose, and it is this purpose that you *must* discover and understand in your own time, as healing takes time!

With the journey comes understanding, and with understanding comes acceptance, acceptance as to whether healing is your path!

HOPE FOR THE FUTURE OF HEALING

One modern day lady who is making a mark for herself in the World of Healing in our present time is *Sandy Edwards*.

She has won a National Lottery Award, and been accepted into today's hospitals. I will consider how she earned the respect of the medical profession to become accepted into hospitals, as this has been a big breakthrough in the acceptance of spiritual healing in our world today.

Looking into the future, I believe that healing will continue to have an important part to play in our futuristic world.

Harry Edwards, in his 1963 book, *The Power of Spiritual Healing,* predicted that healing *would* include *preventative* measures, but we have yet to discover whether his prediction will happen! If past discoveries and Harry's testimonials are anything to go by, the future is looking bright!

Will man continue to extend his life, and what purpose will an extended life have?
Will mankind ever accept the transition from a physical to a spiritual existence, just as if he was taking off an overcoat?
Will the medical profession ever believe in man's spiritual existence?

There is so much hope for the future. I believe we will have to continue to have an open mind to consider and understand the discoveries of our future pioneers of healing.

We should remember, that in Harry Edwards' time, the medical profession would not even consider *spiritual healing*, and now they do!

Consider for a moment what was going through the minds of our ancestors when the simple lightbulb was discovered! The point I am making is that what was once miraculous in the days gone by, is now the norm, and I believe this trend will continue in our World of the Future!

Let's hope that the medical profession, alternative and complementary practitioners will continue to work together, hand in hand, and that the fears of the past WILL disappear...

The purpose of my spiritual books is to distill FEAR of the UNKNOWN.... So let's take one step at a time... breathe in and out... keep an open mind....and let's all begin our healing journey together...

* * *

CHAPTER 2

Past pioneers - Harry Edwards

The purpose of healing is to awaken man's consciousness by demonstrating the power of spirit.

We should not blame God for sickness. If we do blame God for the same, this would mean that God was cruel and ruthless and would make the religion of christianity a nonsense!

— — *HARRY EDWARDS (1963)*

Harry Edwards was born in 1893 and died in 1976. During his lifetime, he made a mark in the history of healing which no one can deny. He knew that he had to prove what he did, as during his lifetime the medical profession did not recognise healing and would disbar any medical personnel who was involved

207

with forms of healing outside of the medical profession. In order to prove his successes, he documented many of his cases, which are detailed and confident.

He believed that the success of spiritualist healing could not have grown so well if it had not of been for the many testimonies of people who bore witness to his successful healings. Some of these people were found to be gravelly ill by the medical profession, and became well again when they received spiritual healing from Harry. These people were from many walks of life!

Harry proved that an anti-faith attitude of his patients did not prevent healing which is why he believed that spiritualist healing outgrew healing by the church, who believed that faith was needed before healing took place. Faith healing will be mentioned in Chapter 8. One example of faith healing is what occurs at Lourdes where many people claim to have been healed from visiting this location.

Harry believed that in order for healing to work, a positive frame of mind was needed, giving the patient inner strength and upliftment. He believed in treating causes and not just symptoms. He states that healing might not be so effective if a patient continued with the reason for the ailment eg if bad eyesight is due to strain at work, and if the patient does not cease the cause, then this would negate the healing process.

Even where complete healing is not possible, there have been cases to prove that minor relief is possible to induce a better sleep or a better passing than was expected by the medical profession. An example of this might be if a patient has a job which is causing him medical problems which he believes should be tackled first.

Another amazing futuristic viewpoint of Harry is that he could see the future of healing, not only to cure diseased, but to prevent it. We all await with bated breath whether his prediction will come true!

He talks about how man is no longer content to accept belief in the church, simply because it is preached to him. It is now 2022, and this message of man no longer being happy to have belief preached to them is still being upheld in modern day literature and coming out of the mouths of modern day mediums, which is where I have heard this message before. I believe this proves how forward thinking Harry Edwards was. *It is possible that this forward thinking claim could have been a spiritual message!*

Harry believed that there was intelligence involved in the act of spiritualist healing, and that this *intelligence* must have a greater wisdom than that of man. If he was correct in this assumption, this would mean that if this intelligence is not human, it must be spirit, which points to the conclusion that there must be a spirit realm! Those who inhabit the spirit realm must therefore have lived human lives. This suggests that there is no death, but a continuance in a new sphere of existence!

Harry believed in the divine purpose of healing and stated that no healer is fulfilling his function unless he tries to point out to his patients the purpose of being a healer. He believed that public services contribute to awakening spiritual consciousness, and he believed that the source of healing is from a heavenly source.

On reading Harry Edward's *'The Power of Spiritual Healing'*, I am very impressed with his knowledge of both spiritual matters and awareness of what is going on in his time, and his hope for the future! I am also impressed with how dedicated that he is to the cause of persuading the world as to the power of healing. It is for this reason that I decided to allow him pride of place in the healing section of this book!

CHAPTER 3

Understanding healing

LOVE is the most important healing power there is.
— LOUISE HAY

Noun:
    Healing is 'The process of making or becoming sound or healthy again': 'The gift of healing'

Adjective:
    Tending to heal; therapeutic : 'a healing experience'; 'the healing process

A t the start of your journey, it is important to understand what *healing* is. You might think you already know this, but since the introduction of complementary methods all around the world, we now all have a vast array of choices, some of which you may know and some of which you may not!

Healing is an ongoing process, and not a 'quick fix'. This applies to all forms of healing! Once one ailment has been *healed*, this does not mean that there will not be other issues to contend with. This is the reason why we all need to be aware of what is happening inside and outside of our own bodies, so that we can seek healing when needed. We need to learn to understand our own energy life force. Only we know what is right for our bodies. What is right for one person, is not right for another!

> *Healers believe that the majority of human afflictions have their primary causations in mental stresses, frustrations, anxiety and soul sickness. Gastric ulcers is an example of this.*
> *Harry Edwards (1963)*

Harry Edwards (healer) said that it was important to discover and treat the underlying cause of an illness first. For example, if you get an occasional headache, try to establish why this might have occurred.

Healing is constantly an ongoing process. Spiritualists believe that our spirit guides constantly need to be reminded that they have a duty to keep us healthy!

CONSIDERING SICKNESS

Sickness is not the will of God. It is wrong to assume that God is the arbiter for the condition of our health. The intervening intelligence must possess a greater wisdom than of man, and if it is not of human origin, then it must come from spirit.
— HARRY EDWARDS (1963)

It does not matter who we are, whether we are healers or not, when we are sick, our mind wonders *why* we are sick, and *who* has made us sick. This is a natural thought process, which we should not feel guilty about. The first thought of many is to blame God for our sickness. However, it would be wrong for us to blame God!

I would suggest that you remind yourself for a second that God was our *creator,* or if you do not believe in God, some other intelligence was our creator! Why would that creator want us to be sick - it just does not make sense!

The creator created.....not destroyeth!

The creator has made us totally in control of our lives, physical and spiritual, and as such we need to be aware of what is happening inside and around us. If we don't feel *complete* we should therefore seek the help of a healer to help us fell whole again.

Many practitioners of different forms of healing talk about the connection between man's mind, body and spirit connection. I will cover this in a Chapter 5, as this in itself is a vast subject.

WHAT DOES HEALING MEAN TO YOU?

Healing can mean many things to many different people. The abundance of explanations is the main reason that I decided to write about the same. It is such a vast area and can easily be misunderstood!

I like my readers to be informed of all the possibilities surrounding spiritual matters, so that they can make their own decisions, and not to force my own beliefs on others. However, as a spiritualist myself, I do believe that we all have personal responsibility for our actions, and as such we should make decisions based on our informed choices.

It is our responsibility to seek out the answers in order to make our informed choices!

It is the seeking out of answers to questions that many don't like to talk about is the main aim of my books!

CHAPTER 4

Medical breakthroughs

The medical profession is at the forefront in healing at the moment which is based on a scientific background. Because of this, it is my duty to guide my readers that if you are ill you should first seek the guidance of the medical profession before you consider any alternative or complementary methods!

We should be grateful of the many breakthroughs in medicine provided by the medical profession. They have made significant breakthroughs which have lengthened our lives, and aided our suffering for generations.

I believe that it is important to consider the pioneers who made important breakthroughs in medicine which have improved everyone's lives, some of which are below.

PIONEERS AND MEDICAL BREAKTHROUGHS

There have been a selection of medical breakthroughs made throughout time which have lengthened our lives and made our lives more enjoyable. Below is a few of these discoveries:

PENICILLIN

History (2006) Sir Alexander Fleming, who was a young bacteriologist, made an accidental discovery which led to one of the greatest developments of modern medicine in 1928. He had left a plate of staphylococcus bacteria uncovered and noticed that a mould that had fallen on the culture which had killed many of the bacteria. He identified the mould as *penicillium notatum*, similar to the kind found on bread. Penicillins are now used to treat a variety of infections such as skin infections, chest infections and urinary tract infections.

VACCINATIONS

The medical profession was reluctant to accept Louis Pasteur's germ theory of disease, primarily because it originated from a chemist. However, during the next decade, he developed the overall principle of vaccination, and contributed to the foundation of immunology. His first important discovery of vaccination came in 1879, and concerned a disease called chicken chorea.

Today, the bacteria that causes the diseases are classified in the *Genus Pasteurella*. It was a chance observation that he discovered *chicken cholera*.

He had inoculated chickens with the attenuated form and demonstrated that the chickens were resistant to the fully-virulent strain. He then directed all of his experimental work toward the problem of immunisation, and applied this principle to many other diseases.

Many discoveries followed on from this discovery. Vaccinations are now regularly used to guard against infections. The latest vaccination that the world was in a rush to create was the one for *Coronavirus!* The United Kingdom was at the forefront in discovering a viable vaccine!

GERM THEORY

In 1860, Louis Pasteur, conducted a series of experiments that showed that microorganisms were responsible for the spoiling of food and the fermentation of wine. He also demonstrated that these microorganisms could cause disease. Today there are tight regulations on the keeping of food and dates now have to be displayed to prevent food poisoning.

ANAESTHETIC

Robin & Toledo (n.d). Conquering pain has been on the forefront of everyone's mind. In 1846 mankind's greatest fear, the pain of surgery was eliminated. In 1846, William T.G. Morton, discovered *Ether.* He proved that if used in the correct dose that it is a safe and effective anaesthetic. Follow on discoveries were made after Morton's first discovery which all contributed to a pain-free surgery.

Today surgeries are possible without the fear of pain during the operation.

ISULIN

Insulin was discovered by Sir Frederick G. Banting, Charles H. Best and J.J.R. Macleod at the University of Toronto in 1927, and it was later discovered by James B Collip. It was one of the greatest medical breakthroughs in history, which went on to save millions of lives around the world and triggered a century of diabetes discoveries. This discovery was only the start of many more discoveries!

DNA

Sun Reporter (2021) DNA is a molecule containing the genetic information to reproduce and grow whole beings. Genetics, however, is not the whole picture of a being, which is further shaped by experiences and environment. An almost identical set of DNA can be found in the nucleus of every cell of the body

The discovery of DNA is as old as life itself, but we have only discovered what it looks like, and how it works over the last 70 years. Lots of scientists, working over many centuries, have been part of the process of helping to understand DNA.

Biologist Friedrich Miescher first identified DNA in a molecule in 1869. He made this discovery by chance in his work on white blood cells. Discoveries followed on by other scientists after this.

DNA is important as it carries genetic information. It has all the instructions that a living organism needs to grow, reproduce and function. It is also used by forensic scientists who use its profile to help solve crimes.

XRAY

History (n.d). In 1895, German scientist, Wilheim Conrad Bonnet (1845-1923) was the first person to observe x-rays, which benefited a variety of fields by making the invisible, visible. His discovery started when he was testing whether cathode rays could pass through glass, when he noticed a glow coming from a nearby chemically coated screen. He named the rays that caused this glow x-rays because of their unknown nature. He learned that x-rays penetrate human flesh, but not higher-density substances such as bone or lead, and that they can be photographed.

X-rays became an important diagnostic tool in medicine, allowing doctors to see inside the human body without surgery. Scientists were quick to realise the benefits of x-rays, but slower to comprehend the harmful effects of radiation. Initially, it was believed that x-rays passed through flesh as harmlessly as light. However, within several years, researchers began to report cases of burns and skin damage after exposure to x-rays.

In 1904, Thomas Edison's assistant, who had worked with x-rays, died of skin cancer. Following this death, scientists began to realise the risks of radiation more seriously.

. . .

THE CIRCULATORY SYSTEM

Zarrinmehr & Schickel (2022) William Harvey was an English physician (1578) who discovered the blood circulatory system of the body through experimentation and theorising. His greatest discovery was that blood flows around the body using a single circulatory system, rather than two separate systems, as previously thought. By circulation, he meant that the blood pumped out is not used up, but comes back to be reused again.

He further reinforced his findings by showing, through a combination of experiments and theories, that it is not possible for the body to produce enough blood to sustain itself if this circulation and reuse of blood does not exist.

HIV

Watson, S (2022). The first reports of strange illnesses started in New York and California in 1981. Healthy young gay men were sickened with *Kapok's Sarcoma*, a cancer usually found in males who were much older. Others were coming down with a rare type of pneumonia. It was found that it destroyed the immune systems, and left the body open to all kinds of infections.

In 1983, scientists discovered the virus that causes AIDS. They later named it *Human Immunodeficiency Virus (HIV)*.

In 2007, the FDA approved the first integrate

inhibitor, *Raltegravir (Isentress)*. This type of drug offers a different way to shortcut HIV from making copies of itself. Today, more than 30 HIV medications are available, and many people are able to control their HIV with just one pill a day.

Early treatment with antiretrovirals can prevent HIV positive people from getting AIDS, and the diseases it causes, like cancer. HIV drugs also stop people who have the virus from passing it to their partner during sex.

There is still not a cure for AIDS, but with the right treatment people who are HIV positive can live a normal live span.

VITAMINS

Casmir Funk (1912) was credited with discovering vitamins, proposed the idea that various diseases could be cured by vita- mins, and during the next few decades, he and other scientists identified various vitamins we know today.

CORONAVIRUS

Crown (n.d). More recently coronavirus has taken the world by storm. Many countries around the world were searching for answers, and no one would admit that they had been responsible for the same. The world was frantically searching for a cure!

In 2020, the world coronavirus treatment was approved for use by the NHS. The government immediately authorised the NHS to use the world's first coronavirus treatment proven to reduce the risk of death. Government trials showed the drug saved lives by significantly reducing the risk of death in hospitalised patients who require oxygen.

A number of vaccines have been produced around the world, but it seems to be mutating as it is a virus, and so regularly versions need to be made to keep pace.

SPIRITUAL GUIDANCE

It is my belief that spirit continues to influence the medical profession. Here is my theory: I would ask you to consider for a moment how spirit have influenced my ordinary life, then consider if they have helped me turn my life around, surely they have aided significant people on the earth plane!

The way that spirit work with me is that when I have a concern on my mind, I ask a question, and I get an answer. In the beginning, I was getting answers to questions in dream state, but now that I have acknowledged spirit, they now help me at any time. However, you have to give spirit permission to help you!

What I am suggesting is that if the pioneers of the medical profession had medical questions on their mind, that it is highly probably that spirit could have guided them, just like they did with me! Spirit even guided Harry Edwards, the late and great healer, by sending messages through various mediums to show him that he was a healer who would change many lives!

· · ·

FINALLY...

Medical breakthroughs, although are wonderful, have increased the need for hospital care because everyone is seeking the cure to their illnesses. Unfortunately, this is putting pressure on the UK's National Health Service, which is now at breaking point!

At the time of writing this book, numerous medical staff are going on strike for pay and conditions.

Once upon a time people would have died from illness, but today, due to the fact that we now have many cures for many illness, lengthening the lives of the masses, means that increased pressure is now on the medical profession. Because of this increased pressure, more and more people are going to be looking for alternative and complementary healing methods, which is the main reason that I decided to write about the place that healing has on our lives around the world!

* * *

CHAPTER 5

Mind, body and spirit

The body, mind and spirit so interact that each part can be affected by the other.
— HARRY EDWARDS (1963)

The part can never be well unless the whole is well.
— SOCRATES 4BC

Let's consider the connection between the mind, the body and spirit to help us understand the same.

(Silver, V. (2009-2021) In the Middle Ages, philosophers did not believe in the mind-body-spirit connection., and believed that the mind and body were separate entities. Our conventional medicine is also based on the model of treating parts instead of the whole person.

. . .

HOLISTIC HEALING - TREATING MIND, BODY & SPIRIT AS ONE

Holistic practitioners believe they can tap into and understand these three elements to seek wellness for their patients. They claim that when you understand all three, you will understand yourself, and hence you will be able to tap into your true desires! Here I am referring to the need to keep your body, mind and spirit healthy and complete.

There are many different types of complementary and alternative healing methods, but they all claim that healing is most effective when you consider the whole person, rather than focusing on specific illness, body parts or symptoms.

Holistic practitioners believe that health is a state of balance, not simply an absence of illness, and that there needs to be an interconnection of mind, body, spirit and environment. This belief has existed for generations.

BELIEFS OF ANCIENT PEOPLE

Ancient people understood that a healthy mind helps create a healthy body, and a healthy body is important to maintain a healthy mind!

When a disruption appears in the body, the cause may trace back to the mind or spirit, in which case. Healing the mind promotes healing of the body. Similarly, a disease in the body can cause disruptions in the mind. These ancient understandings have shaped modern day mind body medicine e.g. medical researchers know that mental stress is a contributing cause behind the majority of diseases.

Ancient people believed that each living being is a connected part of the web of life, and each and every one of us is part of the whole of creation! To strengthen and reinforce this, they took part in rituals to make the mind and spirit work together to heal the body.

In the East, practices such as *chi gong, tai chi, and yoga* developed to reinforce the mind, body and spirit connection.

HOW DO YOU FEEL WHEN YOU FEEL STRESSED?

When you feel stressed, you will notice your physical, mental and emotional symptoms. Consider for a moment the following and you will see for yourself that everything is connected:

What is your body trying to tell you?
What emotions are you experiencing?

When you feel peaceful in your mind, your body is relaxed, you can breathe.

Some people may feel connected to their intuition, and in consequence, more connected to the divine. You may at this time feel inspired to offer gratitude, praise, to sing and dance.

If you feel like you need to dance...dance. If you feel you need to sing...sing.

. . .

MIND, BODY AND SPIRIT CONNECTION
Consider:

When you hurt a part of your body, your whole being is affected. The pain radiates through your entire body, which makes it difficult to think of anything else!

How do you feel when you hear really good news? You feel excited, your body feels supercharged with energy.

Think of how a baby's body responds to everything that happens around them.

WHO IS IN CHARGE - MIND OR BODY?
The non conscious parts of the brain govern automatic biological processes without need of the thinking mind!

Consider emotions:

The brain produces chemicals which go into the body, and affect its functioning e.g. stressful thoughts cause a rise in cortisol, which prepares the body for fright or flight.

Positive thoughts cause a rise in feel-good chemicals that induce relaxation and healing. The thinking conscious mind can cause voluntary responses e.g. you decide to hold your breath. Research is showing that your mind is in your body, and even around your body.

Human intelligence involves much more than the cognitive intelligence of the brain. Not only does the brain communicate with the body, parts of the body communicates with the brain, and so do the microbes living inside us. Each affects the other on a continual basis. Harry Edwards (healer) believed in this *bodily intelligence* also! Great minds think alike!

CELLS

Cell biologists liken cells to miniature people. Since cells have the same systems and receptors as skin, they perceive their environment and the community of cells at large. Their environment is affected by nutrients, toxins, and the perceptions of the individual. This means that our beliefs, attitudes, thoughts, and feelings affect our biology for better or worse. These factors influence how genes express themselves more than DNA. It is not a mature of nature versus nurture, but nurture over nature.

Cells are constantly communicating with each other. They receive information from the brain and energy field responding accordingly. When we experience an emotion, our cells experience the same emotion through energy vibrations and changes in body chemistry. Each cell in the body functions independently, and as a member of the community that makes up your body.

THE HEART-BRAIN CONNECTION

Your heart has thousands of its own neurones that initiate communication with the brain via the *vagus nerve* and vice versa.

In mammals, both brain and heart are involved in receiving, decoding and processing intuitive information. However, it appears that the heart receives this information first.

Unlike Westerners, who place great importance on youngsters to perceive and think with their hearts, only when they are older do they learn to access information with their brains as well!

Heart intelligence explains how coherent, the unity or alignment of the heart with the brain, elicits a peaceful state that positively affects you and others.

Science has also found brain-like structures in other systems throughout the body. The gut is sometimes called the *second brain*. Researchers have also discovered that the billions of microbes residing in the gut and throughout the body may exert the greatest influence over us. They impact the workings of the body and communicate directly with the brain.

THEORY OF UNIVERSAL MIND

It is the soul or spirit, and whether or not it connects to a consciousness beyond ourselves, is debated.

It has been a long-held belief among humans that we have a soul, a part of the Divine within us. This spark connects us to *'all that is'*. It is our true nature, our higher nature. This nature is vibrationally higher than the self-serving, yet necessary, ego. It is our authentic nature of Love.

A popular theory is that your personal local mind is

connected to a universal mind, and that we are all subject to the universal's natural laws.

There are many names for *the universal mind* and the scope attributed to it. Some call it *God*. Others call it *Nature* or the *Universe, the Field*, or *infinite intelligence*. It is believed that this is the realm of all knowledge and our connection to '*all that is*'. It is this universal mind that physics and mediums claim that they connect to.

MIND AND BODY CONNECTION

We have much to learn about harnessing the powerful potential of the mind, body, spirit connection for accessing intuition, healing ourselves, and manifesting our heart's desires. The mind-body works in mysterious, often unpredictable ways.

People who have experienced spontaneous healing know that healing can and does happen without any conscious effort on our part. This is called *the placebo effect*.

The same holds true of people who believe they are cursed. Through the power of the placebo effect, they like zombies, writhe in pain, or be scared to death from a suggestion, and the subconscious belief in its power. Researchers are working hard to solve these mysteries.

In addition to exploring the benefits of heart-brain coherence, recent scientific discoveries on the ever-changing quality of the brain have led to a lot of research on how to rewire the brain for healing, achieving goals, becoming more compassionate, and so on.

. . .

TAPPING INTO YOUR MIND, BODY AND SPIRIT CONNECTION

Individuals and metaphysical practitioners use techniques to access these. These methods vary with skill, the ability to relax and achieve coherence, belief systems, being detached from outcome, and perhaps elements we are not aware of.

Several subconscious mind power techniques are popular tools for deprogramming and shifting outdated pattens and limiting beliefs. They offer new suggestions to your mind, neutralise the charge of troubling emotions so that mental, spiritual, and physical energy can be freed up. Together with mental rehearsal to practice new ways of being and taking action, the brain and body have the energy, circuitry, and experience needed to create a healthier, happier future.

Examples of mind-body manifestation techniques include:

Visualisation Affirmations
Hypnosis
Emotional release techniques
Meditation

Some people use muscle treating or pendulums as a way to access the wisdom of the subconscious for information about anything from which remedies and techniques are best to which foods are harmful, and so on.

. . .

SUMMARY

We have much to learn about how the mind, body and spirit are one, as well as how we are connected to the greater whole.

Although your brain exerts a powerful influence over your body, there is much more to the mind-body connection than a master-slave relationship. The belief that mind powers and levels of consciousness belong to the brain alone is a belief of the past.

The mind, body and spirit connection is more than just a way to get what you want. It is who you are as a wondrous whole being. The philosophy of holistic healing and health makes perfect sense. When you love and are one with your mind, body and spirit, your whole self will benefit, and others will benefit as well!

CHAPTER 6

Positive Thinking

The positive thinker sees the invisible, feels the intangible, and achieves the impossible...

— WINSTON CHURCHILL

Life is a preparation for the future; and the best preparation for the future is to live as if there were none...

— ALBERT EINSTEIN

Love can open all the doors that make all things possible

——DR CHARLES MARSHALL

I have always believed in the importance of positive thinking! I think y0u will find, from an examination of the opinions of all great men in our time, that they too!

From reading the quotes above you will see that two of these men : Winston Church and Albert Einstein also believe in the importance of having a positive mind, and consider what they achieved!

I have also always believed in the importance of loving yourself first, and as soon as you do this, then other people will recognise your love and purpose and will believe in you!

MEDICALLY SPEAKING...

Positive thoughts cause a rise in feel-good chemicals that induce relaxation and healing. The thinking conscious mind can cause voluntary responses e.g. you decide to hold your breath.

Cell biologists liken cells to miniature people. Since cells have the same systems and receptors as skin, they perceive their environment and the community of cells at large. Their environment is affected by nutrients, toxins, and the perceptions of the individual. This means that our beliefs, attitudes, thoughts, and feelings affect our biology for better or worse. These factors influence how genes express themselves more than DNA. It is not a mature of nature versus nurture, but nurture over nature.

Cells are constantly communicating with each other.

They receive information from the brain and energy field and respond accordingly.

When we experience an emotion, our cells experience the same emotion through energy vibrations and changes in body chemistry. Each cell in the body functions independently, and as a member of the community that makes up your body.

Research is showing that your mind is in your body, and even around your body.

Human intelligence involves much more than the cognitive intelligence of the brain. Not only does the brain communicate with the body, parts of the body communicates with the brain, and so do the microbes living inside us. Each affects the other on a continual basis. Harry Edwards (Healer) believed in this *bodily intelligence* also!

So the ending message is......
Keep positive to maintain energy vibrations!

CHAPTER 7

What affects choice?

Although the world is full of suffering, it is also full of over- coming it!

— — HELEN KELLER

This quote by Helen Keller suggests the many ways that healing can be obtained.

It is now important to consider what influences people to choose between different healing methods:

- Opinions of pioneers of the past e.g. Harry Edwards
- Monetary considerations
- Testimonies of patients who claim they have been healed by various methods
- Religious beliefs Spiritual beliefs

- Powerful organisations which provide protection to practitioners e.g. medical profession, Spiritualist National Union
- Desperation when alternative methods have not been successful

TESTIMONIES OF OTHERS

Testimonies of others are very powerful. Harry Edwards was very aware of the need to gather testimonials.

In his day, the medical profession were not allowed to be involved with alternative methods of healing, and could lose their career if they did so. People went to him because traditional medicine had failed to cure them!

In his time, Harry had to balance his wanting to help people with protecting himself, and promoting what he believed in. It is for this reason that he kept very detailed accounts, not only from patients who received contact healing, but also from patients who had received absent healing around the world. Some of the people that sought healing had no faith, but they were still healed which suggests that faith is not needed.

RELIGIOUS BELIEFS AND THE CHURCH

Those who have religious beliefs are tied to these

— DR CHARLES MARSHALL [IN SPIRIT], VIA LESLIE FLINT MEDIUM

Doctor Charles Marshall (in spirit) said, through the mediumship of Leslie Flint (medium), that it was sad that people were tied by their religious beliefs.

To those who have strong religious beliefs, faith can be very powerful. In my opinion, the whole concept of having a positive attitude has to be instrumental in successful healing whether someone has faith or not!

There are religious people and religious places that people frequent for healing. Christians believe that there is a distinct line between faith healing of the church and spiritual healing that is practiced by spiritual healers. Faith healing is an important part of a christian's life. It has been around for decades and mentioned in the Bible, particularly when Jesus was on earth. Today, anyone can be a mediator of faith and give healing to the sick.

Christians believe that if you have faith in God's healing and claim it, you will receive it! Of course, there are a lot of people who no longer believe in the church due to its dogmas and creeds, some of whom feel drawn to the spiritualist religion!

SPIRITUAL BELIEFS

People have been drawn to the religion of spiritualism due to the more relaxed approach that it has with God. Spiritualists believe that faith is not needed in order to be healed. Healing mediums channel God Force energies to their patient and there have been many successful accounts of people who have been healed this way.

OPINIONS OF PIONEERS OF THE PAST

Throughout time, the world has been blessed by people that have made a difference to the world! Harry Edwards was one such a person.

Harry became aware that he was a healer after receiving messages from mediums.In his case, he was spirit led.

I, myself, as a healer, have also been spirit led, as I was not aware of the same until I saw light coming from my hands in a mirror in a darkened room over 12 years ago. As soon as I saw the light, spirit told me that I was a healer so I was never in any doubt. It took me many years however before I felt ready to take up the reins of a spiritual healer!

MONETARY CONSIDERATIONS

This should not be a consideration to your choice of healing, but unfortunately it is!

One such country which is unfortunately influenced by money is the United States of America. It is one of the richest countries in the world, but there are many who do not get the medical treatment that they need due to the fact that they cannot afford to pay for treatment. Due to this financial burden, many have insurance to cover them for medical care, but there are many that cannot afford this insurance and unfortunately they are unable to get the medical care that they need.

The medical profession today is geared towards professionalism, and science today is focused on making money. This was demonstrated when covid hit the world and scientists were fighting to come up with the cure for the same.

Is the medical profession focus on curing the rich leaving the poor unable to afford the medicines that they need?

PROTECTION BY ORGANISATIONS

Faith healing has the protection of the Church. Spiritualist healing has the protection of the Spiritualist National Union. The medical protection has the protection of professional regulators.

When choosing a method of healing, it should always be considered whether there is protection from an organisation who will provide compensation if anything goes amis in your healing. The need for this protection of course increases the more serious the condition is!

DESPERATION WHEN OTHER METHODS OF HEALING. HAVE NOT WORKED

Sometimes people are guided by desperation when

previous methods of healing have not worked. To give an example, in the past women who were desperate to have a termination of their pregnancy were forced to seek the help of backstreet doctors which risked their own lives!

Illness can affect people in many different ways which can make people desperate for a cure!

THE FUTURE AND ACCEPTANCE OF ALTERNATIVE METHODS

The medicine profession believe that you should follow their approach first, and then look to other holistic methods. For the time being, I believe this is the safest approach to take in order for healing to be accepted as the norm in modern society until the medical profession accept other methods of healing,

I believe that Harry Edwards had the right idea by making detailed notes of his successful healings. The reason for this is that alternative methods of healing are more likely to be accepted by the medical profession with proof, and it is only proof that will sway them as to alternative healing methods!

HEALING IS A MIRACLE!

As a final word, I believe that whichever method of healing you choose, healing *IS* a miracle, and that you should let yourself be guided by your own intuition to follow the road to healing which is suitable for your ailment...

CHAPTER 8

Healing options

Healing is universal around the world. Throughout the centuries man has been looking for ways to heal and to extend their lives. I believe they have always known the answer, they just have to look deep inside themselves!

Now that you have a better understanding of your mind, body and spirit connection, and have considered possible causes of an ailment, you will then be

in a better position to consider the many different methods of healing.

I will briefly set out some of the different routes to healing below to give you a starting point for further consideration.

CONVENTIONAL MEDICINE

Some people believe that *healing* can *only* be provided by the medical profession, who have scientific knowledge and resources to cure. The medical profession look to science for the answers, and they believe in *healing* the physical body using their scientific knowledge, medicines and technology. To date, they now recognise spiritual healing, but regard it as *complementary* to medicine, and not *instead of.* They now recognise that sometimes patients need to consider alternative methods of healing when traditional methods have not been successful. Conditions of the mind is one area that they consider alternative methods of healing may be needed. They do, however, urge everyone seeking alternative methods to only go to recognised practitioners who have the backing of professional organisations!

SPIRITUALIST HEALING

Healing energies are channelled from God, through healing guides, to the Healing Medium and finally to the patient. Spiritualists believe that *healing* is directed from the God Force to healing mediums who allow spirit to direct healing to their recipient. In their words:

Healing is from spirit, through spirit, to spirit.

The recipient does not have to have religious beliefs, and the healing medium does not need to know where the recipient's problems lie, as they believe it is the divine who is in control of the same. Spiritualist healing is now recognised by the medical professional as a *complementary* form of healing.

Harry Edwards, was a renown spiritualist healer, and as such, directed energy from the divine. He believed that spiritualists have had the greatest impact on the medical profession which is why it has been recognised by them. This is of no surprise, taking into account the number of testimonies that Harry Edwards has included in his many books! In his books, he mentions that it is important to be aware of the cause of an illness. as this needs to be addressed before healing can continue. He used to like to be kept informed of the progress of his many patients, and kept many detailed records.

REIKI OR ENERGY HEALING

This form of healing is performed by a Reiki Practitioner who uses energy to heal.

Reiki healing practitioners believe they channel universal energy. This is known as 'Ki' (pronounced 'Chi'). This is the same energy involved in Tai Chi exercise. This energy supposedly permeates the body. It is a form of complementary therapy relating to energy healers.

Practitioners believe that they work with energy fields around the body which involves the transfer of universal energy from the practitioner's palms to the client. Many people who have received Reiki claim it has helped them. However, there is some controversy which surrounds Reiki due to the fact that it has not been clinically proven.

Reiki practitioners believe that *energy medicine* aims to help the flow of energy, and remove blocks in a similar way to acupuncture. They believe that by improving the flow of energy around the body can enable relaxation, relieve pain, speed healing and reduce other symptoms.

Reiki practitioners will place their hands lightly on or over specific areas of the client's head, limbs and torso for a short period of time. Some practitioners use crystals and chakra healing wands to enable healing or protect a home from negative energy.

Reiki allegedly aids relaxation, assists in the body's natural healing processes, and promotes emotion, mental and spiritual well-being. As this form of healing is regarded as complementary, it should only be used alongside medical treatment.

FAITH HEALING - THE CHURCH

Faith healing is a form of spiritual healing that occurs when an individual's prayers are answered through divine intervention.

A practitioner of faith healing can be any person who believes in a higher power, and has faith that their prayers will be answered. The purpose of faith healing is to encourage hope, relieve stress, and encourage positive thinking.

The first documented instance of faith healing occurred in the Bible when Jesus healed the sick by laying his hands upon them. Early Christians often used the laying on of hands aa a form of prayer for healing purposes, but this practice was later abandoned by most Christian denominations because it was viewed as superstitious or even pagan-like.

The practice returned to popularity during the 19th century as part of the American Spiritualism movement, and continues today among many religions around the world including:

- Christianity (which also uses conventional medicine)
- Judaism (where prayer is combined with medical treatment,
- Islam (where prayer alone is used)
- Hinduism (where practitioners may use herbs or other natural remedies)
- Buddhism (which uses an array of techniques including meditation); and
- New Age movements such as Reiki (which uses energy manipulation techniques)

PLACES AROUND THE WORLD BELIEVED TO BE HEALING SANCTUARIES

An example of a religious place in the world where faith healing takes place is *Lourdes*.

Lourdes is the city of miraculous healings. The first healings in Lourdes occurred during the Apparitions of 1858. They have not ceased since that time.

The healing of bodies, however, cannot overshadow the healing of hearts. Both the sick and the healthy find themselves in front of the Grotto of the Apparitions: they

are united through the exchange of smiles, through the sharing of gestures and prayers.
    — LOURDES, SANCTUAIRE (N.D)

CHAKRA HEALING

Chakra healing is a holistic practice that involves balancing the energy centres in the body known as chakras.

There are several main chakras in the body, located along the spine from the base to the crown of the head. Each chakra corresponds to different aspects of physical, emotional and spiritual well-being.

Imbalance of chakras can lead to physical and emotional symptoms, such as pain, anxiety, or low self-esteem. There are various ways to balance chakras, and there is a number of ways to do so e.g. meditation, yoga, crystals, sound and colour. Further chapters have been provided going into more depth on chakras and healing chakras using sound and colour (Chapters 9,10 and 11).

ACUPUNCTURE

This is energy healing through touch.

Wong, C. (2022) Acupuncture is a traditional Chinese medicine practice that is based on the idea that a blockage or disturbance in the flow of the body's life energy, which can cause health issues.

Acupuncturists insert thin needles into specific points

throughout the body to balance the body's energy, stimulate healing, and promote relaxation.

Acupuncture may stimulate the release of endorphins, the body's natural pain-relieving chemicals. It may influence the atomic nervous system and needle placement may impact breathing, blood pressure and heart rate.

Acupuncture may be useful for a variety of conditions which include:

- Anxiety
- Arthritis - conditions that involve joint inflammation
- Long-term pain
- Depression
- Insomnia - a condition that involves sleep-related difficulties
- Migraines, which are intense headaches that often include other symptoms
- Nausea
- Sinus congestion or nasal stuffiness
- Stress
- Infertility, which describes a difficulty getting pregnant
- Skin appearance

The health benefits of acupuncture can vary depending on the individual. Bear in mind that it may take several acupuncture sessions before you notice any benefits.

Research on the health benefits of acupuncture is still limited, however, there are some studies that found acupuncture to be helpful for specific conditions.

Prior to getting acupuncture, your consultant will ask about your health history, and may give you a physical examination. During the session, thin needles are placed in specific areas to address your condition or conditions. The consultant may gently twist the needles for added effect. The needles are often left in for 15 to 20 minutes, with the total session lasting anywhere from 30 minutes to an hour. Your consultant may use additional techniques during your session.

As to whether it is painful, you may feel a slight sting, pinch, ache, or some pain as the acupuncture needle is being inserted. Some consultants move the needle after it has been placed in the body, which can cause additional pressure. Once the needle has been properly placed, you may feel a tingling or heavy feeling. It is important to let your consultant know if you are uncomfortable or in a lot of pain at any point during the session, as intense pain may mean the needle has not been inserted or placed correctly.

With regard to side effects, it may cause some side effects in some individuals, which may include:

- Pain and bleeding from the needle insertion
- Nausea
- Infections Skin rash
- Allergic reaction
- Bruising around the areas the needles were placed

- Dizziness

Less common are side effects such as:

- Blood vessel and nerve injury
- Complications from the needle breaking during treatment
- Organ injuries
- Brain and spinal cord injuries.

Whilst rare, acupuncture complications can lead to death. For this reason, it is a good idea to speak with your primary care physician before getting acupuncture, as this treatment may not be right for people with certain health conditions.

In conclusion, researchers aren't exactly sure how acupuncture works, however, theories suggest that it may help release endorphins, as well as influence the autonomic nervous system.

HERBAL MEDICINE

Use of natural herbal medicine to heal illness and bring back the body's state to wellness

Anesa Kratovac (n.d). Healing with herbs is a natural medical art that was used by all ancient societies to heal illness and bring back the body's state to wellness. Herbal medicine was humankind's primary means of healing illness.

Over time, by studying sick animals that grazed on

fields of specific herbs, and how certain herbs interacted with the body, the village healers gathered their knowledge through observation and experimentation.

In all parts of the world, herbs grow wild, and according to the conditions of their environment dictate the types of ailments that are most common within those natural conditions.

Most herbs either grow as common weeds or grow wildly on mountain prairies. The nutritional and healing elements of herbs align with the bodily needs of the population that inhabits specific environments. Mother Nature is wise, and as part of nature, we can become wise by observing her and living according to her cycles!

Various cultures still use herbs for ailments, one of which is the Chinese. Traditional Chinese Medicine fuses the ancient spiritual Taoist philosophy of balance between yin and yang energies with the power of the herbal kingdom. One of the most distinctive aspects of Traditional Chinese Medicine is that it connects the elements of nature to the body's constitution, and has a profound understanding of how specific emotions impact the function of corresponding organs.

All major cultures, with longstanding healing traditions, understood that the energy that we find in herbs and foods is meant to infuse more energy into our system so that it can nourish and heal itself. Void of energy, our cells start to degenerate, and we become ill. Ultimately, herbs provide the energy needed by specific tissues, organs and systems that help to revive their function. In essence, since we are all energy beings, the energy of a plant, herb, or food must make a difference to our well-being. Unlike what most of us have been taught in the West, what we consume energetically does have a profound influence on our health!

Detoxication is the primary step in how we can reclaim our health. By removing toxic obstructions and hydrating and strengthening cells and tissues, we become more resilient, vital and capable to deal with, and even thrive in the modern world. The journey back to health can be hard, given the extent of cleansing we require, but the gifts of the journey are worth every setback!

SUMMARY...

It is important to understand yourself inside and out in order to tackle mind, body and spirit blockages. I have provided another chapter on understanding the connection between mind, body and spirit.

I would conclude by saying that holistic methods of healing seem to be based on imbalance and blockages. Even the medical profession believe in relieving blockages and imbalance, but their beliefs are based on parts of the physical body and not the spiritual body, which holistic practitioners believe in.

CHAPTER 9

Understanding chakras

*A Chakra is an energy centre. In a healthy person, the
chakras work in unison to create life force energy. The
body, mind and spirit benefit from a balance of chakras.*
— *HARRY EDWARDS (1963)*

C hakras have existed backdated 1500 to 1000 BC
with the origin in India. It was first mentioned
in the sacred texts and are also known as *Vedas*
which are an ancient text known to offer spiritual knowledge. Chakra healing is a holistic practice that involves
balancing the energy centres in the body known as chakras.

Bird, H. (2021) There are several main chakras in the
body, located along the spine from the base to the crown
of the head. Each chakra corresponds to different aspects
of physical, emotional and spiritual well-being. Imbalance

of chakras can lead to physical and emotional symptoms, such as pain, anxiety, or low self- esteem.

TECHNIQUES TO BALANCE CHAKRAS

Various ways to balance chakras are:

Meditation : This involves focusing the mind on the breath or a mantra to help quiet the mind and bring balance to chakras.

Yoga : Practising yoga poses can help align and balance the chakras, as each pose targets energy centres in the body.

Crystals and gemstones : Certain crystals and gemstones, such as amethyst or rose quartz are believed to have healing properties that can help to balance the chakras.

Sound therapy : Using sound, such as singing bowls or chanting, can help to resonate the balance of the chakras.

Colour Therapy : Wearing or surrounding oneself with certain colours, such as red for the root chakra or blue for the throat chakra, can help to bring balance to the corresponding energy centre.

Healing the chakras is not a substitute for medical treatment, and it should be used in conjunction with traditional medical care.

Overall, chakra healing is a holistic practice that can help to bring balance and harmony to the mind, body and spirit. It is a powerful tool for personal growth and well-being and can be incorporated into anyone's daily routine.

. . .

UNDERSTANDING CHAKRAS

If you are going to be a healer it is important to understand chakras. The seven main ones help in keeping one's mind, body and spirit in balance. They are energy points in a body that should stay aligned and open. These chakras coordinate within the areas of the body which can affect our overall well-being.

ROOT CHAKRA (COLOUR: RED) (HEALING CRYSTAL: RED JASPER)

Where is it located? It is located at the base of the spine, near the tail-bone

What colour is associated? Red

What is it responsible for? It is responsible for our stability, security and personal strength.

What do we feel when it is balanced and aligned? We feel grounded and connected to the present moment.

What do we feel if this chakra becomes blocked? If this chakra becomes blocked or imbalanced, it can manifest as physical issues such as constipation, colon problems and arthritis.

How do we address blockages in this chakra? To address these issues and maintain overall physical and emotional well-being, it is important to open and align the root chakra through various chakra healing techniques such as meditation, yoga and crystal therapy.

What do we experience by working on the root chakra? We can cultivate feelings of security, stability, and grounding in both our mental and physical states.

What is the healing crystal associated with this chakra? The healing crystal for this chakra is Red Jasper.

SACRAL CHAKRA (COLOUR: ORANGE) (RELATED TO CREATIVITY, PLEASURE AND SEXUALITY) (HEALING CRYSTAL: CARNELIAN)

Where is this chakra located? This is located below the belly button and above the pubic bone.

What colour is it associated with? It is associated with the colour orange, and is related to creativity, pleasure and sexuality.

If this chakra is blocked or imbalanced, how can this manifest? It can manifest as physical issues such as lower back pain, urinary tract problems, and impotence. Emotionally, an imbalance in this chakra may manifest as issues related to self-worth, particularly in regard to creative expression, pleasure and sexual identity.

How to maintain balance in this chakra? In order to maintain balance in this chakra and address any related physical or emotional issues, it is important to work on aligning and opening the sacral chakra through various chakra healing techniques such as meditation, yoga and crystal therapy.

SOLAR PLEXUS CHAKRA (COLOUR: YELLOW) (HEALING CRYSTAL: CITRINE)

Where is this chakra located? This chakra is located in the upper abdomen around the stomach area.

What colour is this chakra represented by? It is represented by the colour yellow.

What feelings are this chakra associated with? It is associated with feelings of confidence and self- esteem.

What can happen when this chakra is blocked? When this chakra is blocked or imbalanced, it can lead to physical issues such as eating disorders, indigestion, ulcers, and heartburn.

What is this chakra also known as? This chakra is also known as the core chakra.

What is this chakra connected to? It is connected to our sense of personal power.

How to maintain balance in this chakra? In order to maintain balance in the solar plexus chakra and address any related physical or emotional issues, it is important to work on aligning and opening this chakra.

What is the healing crystal associated with this chakra? The healing crystal associated with this chakra is Citrine.

HEART CHAKRA (COLOUR: GREEN) (HEALING CRYSTAL: ROSE QUARTZ AND GREEN AVENTURINE)

Where is this chakra located? This is located at the centre of the chest.

What colour is this chakra associated with? It is associated with the colour green.

What does this chakra symbolise? This chakra symbolises love and compassion.

Where is this chakra located? This chakra is the central chakra of the seven chakras.

What is this chakra responsible for? It is responsible for bridging the connection between the upper and lower chakras.

What does this chakra represent? It represents one's ability to love and connect with others.

What happens if this chakra is out of balance? If this chakra is out of balance, an individual may experience feelings of isolation, insecurity, and loneliness. Physical health issues such as asthma and heart problems can also be caused by a blockage in this chakra.

What healing crystal is associated with this chakra? The healing crystals associated with this chakra are Rose Quartz and Green Aventurine.

THROAT CHAKRA (COLOUR: BLUE) (HEALING CRYSTAL: BLUE LACE AGATE AND SODALITE)

What is this chakra associated with? This chakra is associated with communication.

What colour does this chakra represent? It is represented by the colour blue.

What is this chakra connected to? It is connected to verbal communication, and plays a vital role in how we express ourselves.

What happens when this chakra is blocked? It can lead to problems in the throat and its surrounding areas, such as tissues with the gums, mouth, voice and teeth.

What happens when this chakra is properly aligned

and functioning? When this chakra is properly aligned and functioning, an individual will feel compassion and understanding while talking and listening, and will also have confidence while speaking.

Why is it important to keep this chakra balanced? It is important to keep this chakra balanced in order to effectively communicate and express yourself.

What healing crystals are associated with this chakra? The healing crystals associated with this chakra are Blue Lace Agate and Sodalite.

THIRD EYE CHAKRA (COLOUR : INDIGO) (HEALING CRYSTAL: AZURITE)

What is this chakra also known as? This is also known as the brow chakra.

Where is this chakra located? It is located on the forehead between the eyes.

What colour is this chakra associated with? It is associated with the colour indigo.

What is this chakra connected to? It is connected to intuition, imagination, and the ability to see the bigger picture.

What may an individual experience when this chakra is open and aligned? An individual may experience improved intuition, an increased ability to learn new skills, and a stronger connection to their inner voice.

What happens when there is a blockage in this chakra? When there is a blockage in this chakra, it can manifest as physical symptoms such as headaches or hearing problems, and may also cause difficulties with concentration.

CROWN CHAKRA (COLOUR : WHITE OR VIOLET) (CYSTAL: AMETHYST)

Where is this chakra located? This chakra is located at the top of the head.

What colour is this chakra associated with? It is associated with the colours white or violet.

What is this chakra connected to? It is connected to intelligence, awareness and spirituality, and serves as a bridge to an individual's sense of purpose in life.

What happens when the crown chakra is open and aligned? When the crown chakra is open and aligned, it can help to keep the other chakras open and balanced as well, leading to a sense of inner peace and bliss.

What happens when this chakra is blocked? When this chakra is blocked, an individual may exhibit characteristics such as stubbornness, skepticism, and narrow-mindedness.

What healing crystal is this chakra associated with? The healing crystal associated with this chakra is Amethyst.

WHY IS IT IMPORTANT FOR ALL OF THE CHAKRAS TO BE FUNCTIONING PROPERLY

It is important for all of the chakras to be functioning properly in order to achieve overall balance and harmony in the mind, body, and soul. Each chakra is associated with a specific energy point that performs a unique role in maintaining this balance.

Unfortunately, life can often bring challenges and situations that can disrupt the balance of our chakras, leading to the accumulation of negative energy resulting in blockages. Past pain and trauma can be traced back to past pain or trauma that has been stored within them. In order to fully heal and balance the chakras, it may be necessary to confront and release these difficult emotions.

WHAT METHODS ARE AVAILABLE FOR HEALING CHAKRAS?

There are numerous methods available for healing the chakras, including self-care practices such as meditation yoga journaling; and the use of crystals

IN CONCLUSION

It is important for you to find the approach that resonates with you and feels most effective for healing and balancing your chakras. It is also important to eat a healthy diet to maintain inside/outside health.

CHAPTER 10

Chakra healing using sound

Sound healing has been used in healing throughout history. It is used today to assist mental health and to help people work faster and boost morale. It is the use of instruments or voice to release energetic blockages, inducing a state of ease and harmony in the body.
— *NATALIE FARRELL (2022)*

atalie Farrell (2022) Today our modern society uses music to influence mood in our supermarkets to encourage us to spend more, at a funeral to invoke sorrow, and at a wedding to invoke happiness. However, it also has healing properties. It can improve well-being, energy levels and performance at work.

Sound healing is the use of instruments or voice to release energetic blockages which induces a state of ease and harmony in the body. By using singing bowls or chanting, sound can be used to help to resonate the balance of the chakras.

Sound healing synchronises brainwaves to achieve profound states of relaxation, which helps to restore the vibratory frequencies of the cells in our bodies. When vibrations travel through the body, they promote circulation, energy flow and rejuvenation . The frequency of the sound synchronises with the brainwaves and activates distress responses in the body.

Today neuroscientists have discovered that listening to music stimulates a rise of dopamine, which can make us feel good. Practitioners use a combination of instruments such as tuning forks, crystal bowls and gongs which work at different frequencies.

GOING BACK IN TIME....

Pythagoras used the flute and the lyre to heal.

Hippocrates, used sound therapy for his patients with mental difficulties.

Aristotle used flute music to arouse strong emotions and purify the soul.

Aboriginal people have played didgeridoo to reinvade the dreamtime connection.

Sixth century AD India poets sang.

16th century, Bhakti yoga teacher, is believed to have played a key role in developing a form of chanting.

Egyptians understood the properties of sound and used it to aid digestion, treat mental problems and induce sleep. They believed that sound could generate vibrations which had healing properties.

People of Asia also used sound healing. They used singing bowls to induce a state of spiritual awareness and healing.

The Chinese people going back to 11th century also used singing bowls. Today, singing bowls are used in traditional spiritual practices in Asia and by sound healers around the world.

WHAT TYPE OF INSTRUMENTS ARE USED?

Tuning forks are also used to tune instruments, but they have healing powers of their own. These can be held to specific parts of the body to send vibrations which release tension and open blocked energy channels. It is believed that this form of sound healing is good for emotional balance and pain relief.

Gongs are used in gong baths where a practitioner creates different tones and patterns with the gongs to produce vibrations which work on the mind-body connection. These are great for clearing fears or emotional blocks and improving clarity, leaving you transformed on a physical as well as mental level. They can put you in a deeply relaxed and meditative Theta state in as quickly as 90 seconds. Gongs can also be used to stimulate the limbic system (part of the brain involved in our behavioural and emotional responses) forcing your muscles to relax. The sound of a gong is heard through the ears, passing through the auditory nerve and then the vagus nerve, stimulating every organ in the body. All your organs will operate more effectively, especially your liver and kidneys. You wake feeling refreshed and invigorated!

Singing bowls produce a deep sound that relaxes and heals the mind. They can also work on various parts of the body. They elicit a light dream state and can be placed on the body to promote healing. This type of sound healing has been found to reduce stress, anger, depression and fatigue.

THE BENEFITS OF SOUND HEALING

It is believed that sound healing can help you clear energy blockages, and thus facilitate healing on a physical and mental level. Some of the benefits include reduced stress levels, fewer mood swings, lower blood pressure, lower cholesterol and improved sleep. Over the years, it has been used to treat a number of conditions including anxiety, depression, post-traumatic stress disorder, autism and dementia.

USING FREQUENCIES FOR HEALING

Solfeggio frequencies is a form of music with sound patterns to stimulate the brain. These frequencies are typically used for transformational purposes, and can help improve relationships, deal with fear and change, awaken one's intuition, etc. These tones contain a frequency to balance your energy and heal you.

Binaural beats frequency is often used as chill out

music and found in meditations. These can be used for a variety of purposes such as meditation, lowering stress levels and anxiety, increasing focus, relieving pain and aches, improving sleep and overcoming depression.

Vocal toning is a type of sound healing which involves using one steady tone to open your energetic pathways. Using a specific tone allows you to access a particular point of the body and begin to heal it.

The voice is the only tool more powerful than the gong, especially your own voice, because you are self-generating the healing vibrations to shift energetic blocks. That is why many mantras are so powerful as they harness the energetic capacities of the ancients from the Egyptians and Greeks to indigenous tribes.

CONCLUSION

Sound definitely has healing qualities! From my own personal experience, spirit definitely communicate with me at a deeper level when I listen to music. Listening to the right kind of music is also important! I have also noticed myself the effects of talking to patients after giving healing appears to be very beneficial, some would say more beneficial!

* * *

CHAPTER 11

Chakra healing using colour

Colour healing has an important role in getting and staying healthy. Just as our bodies need food and water to survive, it also needs colour or light to balance and energise, because colour is light, and light is an essential nutrient to life.

— ELMARIE SWATZ (2006-2023)

Looking back through history, healing with colour has been practised throughout the western world for decades, going back 5,000 years. Most of the knowledge surrounding the use of colour for healing has been passed from one generation to another, with each culture having their own beliefs on the properties of different colours.

The ancient Egyptians wore amulets of coloured stones:

RED to treat disease and build strength
YELLOW to increase happiness
GREEN to improve fertility

The physical body is an instrument that registers your mental, emotional and spiritual imbalances following from conscious or unconscious mind. A healing practitioner may assist your recuperation, but your healing must come from within!

Disease begins in the auric field, and if not treated at this level, will eventually manifest as a physical disease. If only the physical ailment is worked with, and not the cause, the physical symptoms will continue to manifest. An example of this is eczema.

People who have the gift of auric sight, or who can feel the aura, use vibrational energies of colour for various ways of healing.

Colour healing is where you concentrate your thoughts to where energy will go. By concentrating on a particular healing colour through visualisation, the energy of that colour will be projected by your thoughts. Every day, your body regenerates healthy cells and unhealthy cells, and colour healing is a good way to keep your body balanced. There are many ways to heal with colour. The best way is the way that works best for you!

Colour healing therapy can be used with success as the therapist works with the physical disease as well as dealing with the emotional cause of the disease. High levels of stress, trauma or suppressing strong emotions over a period of time can eventually cause skin disorders eg suppressed anger can affect organ systems that have direct links to the quality and health of the skin. Harry Edwards, Spiritual Healer, also believed in the importance of treating the cause.

THE BEAUTY OF COLOUR

It is so easy to introduce colour into your life by simply changing clothes, so why should you not try for yourself whether certain colours make you feel more balanced!

CHAPTER 12

Spiritualist healing

WHAT IS SPIRITUALIST HEALING?
Healing energies are provided by the God Force and healing mediums act as channels to direct healing energy to their patient. The healing medium places their hands on the shoulders of their patient, with their consent, connecting to the God Force, and passively allowing energies to flow through them to provide healing..

In Law, spiritualist healing, is regarded as a complementary therapy, which means that it is not intended to replace traditional medicine.

Most people make their first point of contact with a spiritual church when they go for healing. A healing medium is not doing their job properly if they do not help their patients understand the philosophy of spiritualism when they come for healing. The philosophy of the same is based on the 7 principles.

It is important for the spiritualist healer to set intention with the definite when focusing on attunement with their patient. A thought directive is the common factor that links all spiritual healing, no matter from which source it arises. Intermediaries in spirit are the actual healing agents to which a healer can establish attunement.

Harry Edwards mentions that it is important to be aware of the cause of the illness as this needs to be addressed before healing can continue. He says that he likes to be kept informed of progress by his patients. However, the Spiritualist National Union says that the medium does not need to be aware of the illness of the patient as the spiritual team will be aware of the same and Healing Mediums just need to be a channel.

WHAT HAPPENS WHEN YOU ENTER A SPIRITUALIST CHURCH FOR HEALING

When you enter a place of healing, if this is your first time, you will be shown a What Happens Next Card which demonstrates the areas of contact and asked if you agree to contact in these areas. You will also be asked to complete a patient record to confirm that you understand that healing is complementary to medicine.

All information completed on this form will be held in strict confidence, and only allowed to be kept for a requisite number of years.

You will be directed to a comfortable chair usually in a circle and the healing mediums will work around the circle, going from patient to patient. During the healing session, relaxing music may be played and prayers will be said.

After the healing session, you will be asked how the healing was for you, and this information will be entered onto the patient record card.

TYPES OF SPIRITUALIST HEALING

There are 3 types of spiritualist healing: contact, distant and absent. Below are more detailed explanations of these 3 types of spiritualist healing.

CONTACT HEALING - The healing medium is in the same room as the patient and makes contact by placing their hands on the shoulders or back of the patient, with their consent.

DISTANT HEALING - The healing medium is either in the same room as the patient at a distance or in the patient's presence via zoom. You will be sent a zoom link if you request this option.

ABSENT HEALING - Here the patient requests if healing energies can be sent to someone in need. It arises from thought processes as far as the healer is concerned. Harry Edwards believed that absent healing was just as effective as *contact healing*. He documented this in his many books.

TRAINING TO BE A SPIRITUALIST HEALING MEDIUM

If you are interested in becoming a spiritualist healing

medium, you should contact the Spiritualist National Union, the contact details which are at back of this book in the Bibliography.

CHAPTER 13

Am you a healer?

The gift of healing is personal, and not professional. No one can be an instrument for healing unless he feels an inner yearning, in sympathy, love and compassion. The healing gift must come from the heart!
— HARRY EDWARDS (1963)

Healers often do not know that they are a healer until someone visits them requesting healing and then later reports of the relief that they believed they received from the healing medium. Harry Edwards only knew he was a healer when various mediums told him of the same.

It is not necessary to be a spiritualist in order to be a healer, nor is it necessary to be religious, the mere allowing healing energies through yourself does, according to many, allow healing to be performed. There have also been instances of healers asking for healing for themselves, and having a profound result.

There are some accounts of laying hands on affected areas, and other accounts where healers just place hands on shoulders, allowing the healing forces to seek out the affection. It would seem that the mere willingness to help others with a positive frame of mind seems to be the way forward, setting intention.

SIGNS THAT YOU MAY BE A HEALER

Power of Positivity (2017) You feel guided in your life. Your guidance not only comes from your own intuition, but from others.

You are empathic and sensitive, and sometimes feel that you want to heal the world.

You spend most of your time alone. The reason for this is that the noise and pain of the outside world can sometimes be too much.

You feel you have a calling to help people and the planet.

People come to you all the time for advice as they feel at ease with you.

You're deeply in touch with your intuition. You suffer from anxiety and/or depression. The pain from the outside world can sometimes become too much for you.

Social interaction exhausts you. You attract others to you who feel that you can help them.

You are drawn to healing techniques or professions.

You do not understand why you are attracted to different healing techniques or professions. You just are!

MY HEALING JOURNEY

The beginning of my healing journey started when I saw light shining from my hands in a mirror, hung in a darkened room, over 12 years ago, during my first unfoldment.

Along my journey, many mediums told me that I was a healer, but it took 12 years and a lot of self-discovery before I was ready to take on the role as a spiritualist healer. It was only when I fully understood the same, did I wish to share with the world the true beauty of healing, and the part that it plays in combining mind, body and spirit as one.

At the beginning of my journey, I can remember going to healing sessions, receiving healing myself, and watching others receive healing. Although I had always believed in the divine, I found it hard to believe that healing actually took place! So I must ask myself what made me eventually believe in healing, and what made others believe in me! The only answer that I can come up with is my positivity, but deep down I realise that something much deeper happened to me, and it is this that I am aiming to discover which I will share with you. Various people also told me that they feel drawn to me to help them.

Since I started my healing journey, people told me that they had noticed changes within me: more confidence, more positivity. The side of me that they did not see, however, is that I would have to occasionally make time for myself to connect to the divine. This meant that I now had a more solitary life, which I knew was the price that I had to pay, but despite this, I knew that what I would receive in return would far outweigh what I was giving...

FINALLY...

Do not think there are too many healers in the world. If you have a calling to be one, then you should be one!

CHAPTER 14

Past, Present & Future

"*Freedom is not worth having if it does not include the freedom to make mistakes.*"
MAHATMA GANDHI

Fom this quote you can glean that we all have the freedom to examine different pathways; and if we did not make mistakes along the way we will not recognise right from wrong.

It is important, I believe, to now consider various ways of inner healing. As I have said previously, it is important to know your inner self (spiritual) as well as your physical self.

To consider the part that you can play in your own healing:

Are you ready to move on from your past?
Accept how this has lead you to your present.

Prepare a blueprint for your future

By understanding our spiritual as well as our physical make-up, you will be in a better place for our tomorrows...

HOW DEEP IS YOUR PAIN? PAST LIVES REGRESSION?

We all have fears and phobias, some more than others, but why do we have these when we must know that they will only hold us back in the future, almost like we want to torture ourselves. Have these fears and phobias been created from our own life experiences, or do they go further back than this to previous lives?

CONSIDERING MY DEEP ROUTED FEARS

Let's consider some of my own life experiences here:

- I have always had a fear of deep water. My father taught both my son and I to swim in the same way, at the same place. Why did my son grow up to be totally fearless of water, but I developed fear of the same, which has remained with me my entire life. One holiday time, I watched in awe as he rode the waves in an artificial sea environment in *Disney World*, Florida as if he was a professional surfer.
- Why did I always have deep religious beliefs when I was not bought up in a non-religious environment. My son, in comparison, has

grown up to not have any religious beliefs, so far! He must have come to this conclusion himself, as both his parents never influenced this.

- Why was I, from a young age, obsessed with life after death and would find every opportunity to watch films, read books on the same and enjoy talking to people about my beliefs which would often shock friends and family!

- Why did my mother admit that the only thing she was scared of in life was *death*, which I only found out when she confessed this through the mediumship of Jean Kelford. I believe that she felt this way because she had no belief that there was an existence after life, and she believed that *the end was the end!* A short while before my mother passed she sat quietly, and most uncharacteristically said: *'What is going to happen to me?'*. I knew that she did not believe in spiritual matters like me, but I had to answer her question to the best of my ability. I kept my answer simple and told her that she would leave her body. In reply she said: *'Oh well, that's it then'*. From this brief uncharacteristic conversation between us, she did not question further, and we continued our usual chit chat of life's events. When Jean Kelford relayed that my mother said that she suspected something towards the end of her life, she thanked me for relaying this information to her which she said helped her understand what was going to happen to her at the end of her life. No one knew what my mother said at this time. This message was from mother to daughter. What had made her so scared of death? Was it her earthly experiences that made her feel this way, or was this a past life experience seeping through.

If it is past lives that we are remembering, they appear to be deep routed in our minds, and we only appear to remember the same when the occurrences happen in our lifetime. We are perplexed why we are so scared, all that we know is that we *ARE* scared!

Some people believe that we have past lives to deal with, and that we are living our present life to help others with the knowledge that we gained from a previous life.

CONSIDERING PAST LIVES - REGRESSION

Some people believe that when we have deep seated pain that sometimes this can be as a result of a past life issue. Sometimes where pain is so deep you might need the help of a hypnotist or past lives regression therapist to help you get to the route of the problem.

I am a great believer in tackling the past as that is what I had to do to sort myself out!

* * *

CHAPTER 15

The future of healing

'Does alternative and complementary methods of healing have a place in modern medicine?'

To answer this question, I think we need to consider the many thousands of people around the world that have been cured by many different healing methods. Each of these people are individuals in every way, and each have their own unique story to tell!

I do not think that there is just one method of healing per se. Each one of us has a unique energy system, therefore to generalise all symptoms, properties and cures into one category is a disservice to individuals and humanity as a whole. For that reason, I believe that we all need to understand why things have happened in our past that have caused you to be in the position that you are in today which might help you consider which healing method is right for you.

Following on from this, if you do not understand your past, how can you possibly understand your future! You need to know yourself inside and out in order to choose the correct healing that you believe is going to work for you. Only you know yourself inside and out so don't be afraid to discuss with holistic practitioners whether certain healing methods are for you!

I strongly believe that healing is the way to go for the future.

Harry Edwards in his book published in 1963: *The Power of Spiritual Healing* also agrees with me on this point. He could see a time when healing would be used for preventative treatment as well as the healing of a condition!

CHAPTER 16

Healing in the Spirit World

The idea of mankind being guided suggests to me that pioneers of the past had a definite purpose to help mankind move forward. If I am right, and this purpose exists, then we will continue to have pioneers of the future who might achieve who knows what, who knows when! We can only hope and dream for a better tomorrow!

From listening to the recordings of Leslie Flint, who was a physical medium, who used to bring through spirits via a voice box above his head, it is clear that our earthly knowledge is not wasted in the afterlife. There are accounts where people who were doctors on the earth become doctors in the afterlife, but instead of curing physical ailments, they cure spiritual issues. They talk about where people are steadfast in their beliefs and headstrong, they are often the most difficult to cure!

There is mention of spiritual hospitals, where those who have spiritual baggage from their lifetime are tended to. So, it seems that healing does not stop in this world, it continues in the world thereafter! One man tending another, and by doing so, strengthening their own spiritual path!

From the spirit recordings of Leslie Flint, many people come back to say how beautiful the colours are in the spirit world, how the flowers don't need to be tended, they are just naturally beautiful! From this, it is clear that colour therapy is an important part of spiritual healing, and part of life as we know it!

Acknowledgments

I have made many friends along my spiritual journey, but the following 3 people have been prominent in my life: Dorothy Cole, Vice Principal, Sutton Cold!eld Spiritualist Church, Nicola Green (my oldest school friend); and Lisa Twinks-West (who I first met at Erdington Christian Spiritualist Church). Without their help I could not have come as far as I have!

Epilogue

By putting together my three books Spirit Writer, Pure Spirit and Spirit Healer has given me a chance to remember how far I had come in my spiritual journey. Sometimes it is so easy to forget how far you have come and need reminding!

*I think the most important lesson I have learnt on my journey is to remember that none of us are alone!
We are all here for a purpose! You may think that purpose only concerns you, but remember how our ancestors have been guided by spirit!*

Our lives.....our futures.....are spun together like a spider's web!

Sweet dreams....hold love in your heart and remember are NOT alone, your loved ones walk beside you every day, now and forever more!

Bibliography

Arthur Findlay College (2018) (Psychic and Mediumship Course)
Https://www.arthurfindlaycollege.org
Viewed: 16th May 2022

Baker, A. (President of the Havant Spiritualist Church)

Beetlejuice (1988) (Film)

Bible, The: Acts 2:4

Bible, The King James Version (2022) [Online]
Available at https://www.kingjamesbibleonline.org/Luke-Chapter-10/
Viewed: 22nd October 2022

BIG Spiritual (2023) (What Is Spiritual Healing?)

Bird, H. (2021) (Chakra Healing: A Beginner's Guide To The 7 Chakras)

Crown (n.d) World First Coronavirus Treatment Approved For Use By
    Government

Eckhart, T (2020) (The Beginning of Awakening and Essential Identity)
https://www.youtube.com/watch?v=S_o2iOavxYI
Viewed: 15th April 2022

Edwards, H. (1963) The Power of Spiritualist Healing, Herbert Jenkins
    Ltd.

Farafan, A. (2017) THE UNEXPLAINED Scientists 'prove' that the
    should does not die: It returns to the UNIVERSE
https://www.linkedin.com/pulse/unexplained-scientists-prove-soul-
    does-die-returns-universe-%D8%AA%D8%A7%D8%B1%D8%A7%
    D8%AA/
Viewed: 15.4.2022

Farrell, N. (2022) (Sound Healing with Song, Gong, Music & More),
    Psychic News December 2022

Ghost (1990) (Film

History (n.d) German Scientist Discovered X-rays

History (2006) (Penicillin Discovered By Sir Alexander Fleming)

100huntley (2020) (Doctor has near-death experience that transforms his
    life)

https://www.youtube.com/watch?v=sv0ZPnXU-9E

Viewed: 2nd May 2022

Kelford, J. and Beech, C. International Mediums

Kratovac, A. (n.d) (Healing With Herbs: Herbs As Medicine And How To Use Them For Body Detox) Red Grape Wisdom

Leslie Flint Trust, The (1997-2022) (Harry Price)

https://leslieflint.com/harry-price

Viewed 15.4.2022

Lourdes, Sanctuaire (n.d)

National Spiritualist Association of Churches (2016- 2022) (9 Principles)

https://nsac.org/

Viewed: 25th May 2022

NourFoundation (2014) (Do Atheists have Near-Death Experiences?) The New York Academy of Sciences

https://www.youtube.com/watch?v=rUfW_Ek54sA

Viewed: 1st May 2022

Power of Positivity (2017) (10 Signs You're Meant To Be A Healer)

Ray Wilson Healing Sanctuary (formerly of Erdington Christian Spiritualist Church)

https://www.facebook.com/profile.php?id=100091552989613

Robinson, D.H. & Toledo, A.H. (n.d) (Historical Development of Modern Anaesthesia)

Rogers, J. (Medium and Author of *Simply Spiritual)*

Sadhguru (2012) (Dimension Beyond the Physical)

https://www.youtube.com/watch?v=WJWXf2A0Nb4&t=1s

Viewed: 16th May 2022

Silver, V. (2009-2021) (The Mind Body Spirit Connection) Holistic Mind Body Healing

Sixth Sense, The (1999) (Film)

Spiritual Experience (2022), The Pure Spirit [Online] Available at

Https://spiritualexperience.eu/pure-spirit

Viewed: 22nd October 2022

Spiritualists' Nationalist Union (n.d) Our Philosophy & the Seven Principles [Online]

https://www.snu.org.uk/7-principles

Viewed: 22nd October 2022

Spiritualists' National Union (n.d) (SH1 Accreditation Level Course)

https://www.snu.org.uk/faqs/becoming-an-approved-healer
Viewed: 14th June 2023

Sun Reporter (2021) (GENE-IOUS Who Discovered DNA?)
https://www.thesun.co.uk/news/15702401/who-discovered-dna/
Viewed: 14th June 2022

Sutton Coldfield Spiritualist Church, Kenelm Rd, Sutton Cold!eld, B73 6HD Phone: 0121 354 3266
https://scsconline.co.uk/

Watson, S. (2022) (The History of HIV Treatment: Antiretroviral Therapy & More), Web MD

What Dreams May Come (1998) (Film)

Wong, C. (2022)'T(the Benefits And Side Effects Of Acupuncture) Very-WellHealth

Zarrinmehr, S. & Schickel, T. (2022) (William Harvey: Physician, Anatomist And The Discoverer Of Blood Circulation), Study.com
https://study.com/learn/lesson/william-harvey-accomplishments-blood-circulation-discovery.html